Praise for *A Resurrection*

D0444036

"Jake Owensby's *A Resurrection-Shaped Life* took my breath away—each personal story, each story from the Bible, and each story of our conflicted days proclaims the truly good news that healing, freedom, justice, and joy can be learned by walking the way of Jesus. There are myriad books on following Jesus, but none like this one. Every page sings with intelligence, insight, and inspiration. It made me remember what kind of human I long to be—and why I can't quit Jesus. Read *A Resurrection-Shaped Life* and fall in love again with God—and with hope."

—**Diana Butler Bass**, author of *Grateful*

"Christ is risen! And yet sorrow, anger, shame, and failure, writes Jake Owensby in this generous book, are also part of every resurrection. Through intimate stories and open-hearted reflections on the gospel, Owensby tenderly shows us how to enter, just as we are, into Jesus' promise of new life. 'People with dirty feet wash people with dirty feet,' he points out. 'Eternal life starts here.'"

—**Sara Miles**, author of *Take This Bread*, *Jesus Freak*, and *City of God*

"Too often, as we attempt to live out the Christian narrative, we use the resurrection to slap a smiling face onto our bitter mourning. Yet, in the beautiful, wise words of *A Resurrection-Shaped Life*, Bishop Jacob Owensby allows the grief to break and form us, which brings startling insight to our resurrected beliefs."

—**Rev. Carol Howard Merritt**, pastor and author
of *Healing Spiritual Wounds*

"In *A Resurrection-Shaped Life*, Jake invites us into a conversation about what it means to truly live resurrection. If you're looking for a beautiful book that infuses the lovingkindness of Jesus with the realness of our humanity, this is the book for you!"

—**Kaitlin Curtice**, author of *Glory Happening*

"Beware: *A Resurrection-Shaped Life* is addictive—as a tonic, not an opiate. This book will not help you escape your problems but will coach you to wrestle with great expectations. Owensby applies to our brokenness the Japanese art of kintsugi, mending with fine gold the scars of broken pottery. He finds God in 'messy places.' Spirituality does not rescue us from the world but sends us smack dab into its midst to serve those with greatest need. Faith has political consequences. Owensby dares to love the world, all of it, as God loves it."

—**Louie Crew Clay**, Professor Emeritus, Rutgers University

"In his new book, *A Resurrection-Shaped Life*, Bishop Jake Owensby celebrates the transformative power of resurrection in all its manifestations in our daily lives. With clear, compelling examples from Scripture, literature, and his own astounding memoir, he explores the ways Christians are renewed, rewarded, and called to 'shed a false and probably toxic image of themselves in order to become their true selves' via this holy, ongoing work. His message is straightforward and his call for a rededication to another holy pursuit—justice—is a splash of cold water, refreshing and thought provoking. This book will make you pray and reflect and gives context for the trajectory of the Christian journey: not a bullet-straight path to heaven but a continual dying and rebirth in a fragile soul, beloved of the Father. You will finish it challenged and reassured."

—**Janis Owens**, author of *American Ghost*

"Hope is more than optimism. Hope is knowing that God is making out of the mess of life something honest, beautiful, and transforming. Life is shaped like Resurrection. What a thrilling wonder! Thanks, Jake, for the reminder."

—**The Right Rev. Robert C. Wright**,
Bishop of the Episcopal Diocese of Atlanta

"The Gospel promises not only that Jesus saves us but also that he transforms us. In *A Resurrection-Shaped Life*, Bishop Jake Owensby maps just what a life transformed by God's grace looks like. This book is insightful, delightful, and a message of hope."

—**Carl McColman**, author of *The Big Book of Christian Mysticism*
and *Answering the Contemplative Call*

A
Resurrection
SHAPED LIFE

DYING AND RISING ON PLANET EARTH

JAKE OWENSBY

Abingdon Press
Nashville

A RESURRECTION-SHAPED LIFE

DYING AND RISING ON PLANET EARTH

Copyright © 2018 by Abingdon Press

All rights reserved.

No part of this work may be reproduced or transmitted in any form or by any means, electronic or mechanical, including photocopying and recording, or by any information storage or retrieval system, except as may be expressly permitted by the 1976 Copyright Act or in writing from the publisher. Requests for permission can be addressed to Permissions, The United Methodist Publishing House, 2222 Rosa L. Parks Blvd., Nashville, TN, 37228-1306 or emailed to permissions@umpublishing.org.

Library of Congress Cataloging-in-Publication Data

Names: Owensby, Jacob, 1957- author.
Title: A resurrection-shaped life : dying and rising on planet Earth / Jake Owensby.
Description: Nashville : Abingdon Press, [2018] | Includes bibliographical references.
Identifiers: LCCN 2018015941 (print) | LCCN 2018042581 (ebook) | ISBN 9781501870828 (ebook) | ISBN 9781501870811 (pbk.)
Subjects: LCSH: Christian life. | Spiritual formation.
Classification: LCC BV4501.3 (ebook) | LCC BV4501.3 .O964 2018 (print) | DDC 248.4—dc23
LC record available at https://urldefense.proofpoint.com/v2/url?u=https-3A__lccn.loc.gov_2018
015941&d=DwIFAg&c=_GnokDXYZpxapTjbCjzmOH7Lm2x2J46Ijwz6YxXCKeo&r=ox0wiE5w
yqlD4NWBvXI_LEW57Ah1_xv-dTElReAYRyw&m=B4EbdTKNcDfOoXC2XS2wmPBCIO_Thw
ejo4XT20pvlXE&s=L1lkc4djSxvbbWz-WAiuCxEQWUIOLUtwWP_AvQjfY9I&e=

Scripture quotations are from the New Revised Standard Version Bible, copyright © 1989 National Council of the Churches of Christ in the United States of America. Used by permission. All rights reserved worldwide. http://nrsvbibles.org/.

18 19 20 21 22 23 24 25—10 9 8 7 6 5 4 3 2 1

MANUFACTURED IN THE UNITED STATES OF AMERICA

For Joy
my favorite person ever

To lie flat on the ground with the breath knocked out of you is to find a solid resting place. This is as low as you can go. You told yourself you would die if it ever came to this, but here you are. You cannot help yourself and yet you live.

—Barbara Brown Taylor, *An Altar in the World*

The most amazing fact about Jesus, unlike almost any other religious founder, is that he found God in disorder and imperfection—and told us that we must do the same or we would never be content on this earth.

—Richard Rohr, *The Naked Now*

CONTENTS

PRELUDE

The world breaks everyone and afterward many are strong at the broken places.

—Ernest Hemingway, *A Farewell to Arms*

In *A Farewell to Arms*, Ernest Hemingway makes a bleak and tragic point about how the world crushes and kills even the best among us. And there is no question that the world we inhabit takes its toll on our tender hearts and fragile bodies.

But if we substitute one word, this line crystallizes the meaning of the resurrection: "The world breaks everyone and afterward many are beautiful at the broken places." Hemingway's use of "strong" conveys that those who survive the world's brutal treatment have scars to show for it. Their scars tell the story of what they have endured. Scar tissue is strong, but it is disfiguring. By replacing "strong" with "beautiful," I'm encouraging us to look for what God does with the broken places of our lives. The message of the resurrection is that God transforms the life we are actually living— sorrow, wounds, regrets, and all—into symbols of love's power to mend and to heal. Just look at what Matthew tells us about Jesus's resurrection (Matthew 28:1-10).

In the predawn light of the third day, the two Marys—Mary Magdalene and the other Mary—crept through the fading shadows to see Jesus's tomb. An angel was loitering at the scene, perched on the stone that he had rolled away from the entrance. He said, "You are looking for Jesus who was crucified. He is not here; for he has been raised" (Matthew 28:5b-6). It was a lot for those two to take in. It's a lot for me to take in, to be honest. The angel is saying something like this: "If you're looking for Jesus's battered corpse, you're just not going to find it. It's not here. It's not anywhere. His corpse hasn't been moved. It's been transformed. Jesus isn't a corpse anymore."

You can catch up with him in Galilee, but don't go looking for the pre-crucifixion Jesus, either. Once you lay eyes on him, you can see for yourself. Nails leave a mark, after all. Just like everything else. What Jesus endured made him who he is. But none of that disfigures him. Grace has been at work. God has mended him. The wounds of the cross are woven together with all that unique stuff that makes Jesus, well, *Jesus*: the tender moments on his mother's knee, candlelit dinners with Mary Magdalene, fishing with Peter and Andrew, embracing a startled leper. Grace has done its finest, most surprising work yet. Grace has mended the fragile body of Jesus.

As the late Marcus Borg put it, the Christian life follows the pattern of the resurrection: dying and rising.[1] The resurrection is not merely something that happened to Jesus two millennia in the past. Neither is our own resurrection something that happens to us only after we draw our last breath. Jesus's resurrection is shaping our everyday, ordinary lives. God's best work is happening right now in the broken places of our lives. That's what it means to experience a resurrection-shaped life.

In *Hallelujah Anyway*, Anne Lamott briefly compared grace to the Japanese art form Kintsugi.[2] I think Kintsugi is an especially apt illustration for a resurrection-shaped life. Kintsugi is the art of repairing broken pottery. Artisans mend the chips and cracks of bowls and saucers, pitchers and jars using lacquer mixed with gold dust. Initially you might assume that the artists are trying to disguise the damage to a piece of pottery by covering it with gold leaf. But these artists aren't trying to hide anything. They realize that the gold-infused lacquer will effectively draw the eye to the very places where the object has been cracked. They intend to highlight the broken places. Beauty emerges from the distinctive broken places of each individual object.

Here in the West, we've received the Greek notion of beauty. We prize flawless harmony and proportion. Blemishes diminish the value of a work of art. Not so for the Japanese. Wear and cracks and breaks tell the story of each unique thing's life. Beauty is not found in something's original, pristine condition; an object's value lies in the life it has lived. And living always comes with some wear and no small amount of damage. Rather than hide the broken places from us, the Japanese artists want us to recognize that we are looking at a broken object that has been mended. Mending a fragile thing reveals the deep love that its owner has for the object. It is held too dear to discard, no matter how much damage it has endured. And crucially, mending a broken thing makes it even more beautiful than it was in its original, unblemished state.

Analogously, grace is already molding and shaping our life right here on planet Earth. In the beginning, grace brings into being a universe of tender, fragile things. Grace abides with these delicate, vulnerable creatures as they grow and mature. As they pass from youthful powers to fading sight, hairy ears, and turkey necks. As they stumble and gasp for breath and howl from the pain of wounded flesh and shattered hearts. "God never intended for the fragile things of this world to retain the pristine condition of a newborn. The living God means for us to live. And living inevitably brings with it wear and breakage. And so grace reaches its climax by mending fragile, beloved things. That's what we mean by resurrection. In the resurrection, God mends the shattered Jesus. And in Jesus' resurrection, we see the promise of our own."[3]

Now, of course, the resurrection points to life after this life. When we breathe our last, our life—our whole life—will continue on the far shore of eternity—mended. But that mending gets its start already right here on planet Earth. Sometimes it happens in three days. Sometimes it happens in three hours or three weeks or three decades. Christ mends the wounds inflicted on us by strangers and lovers, by family and friends, even by the blunt-force trauma we've managed to give ourselves.

None of this is magic. The really big mending projects take a lot of time and no small amount of cooperation by us. And if the truth be told, a lot of our most important mending will continue when we pass from this life to the next. In the meantime, Jesus would very much like it if we handle ourselves and each other with care. We are all terribly fragile and already more than a little damaged, but God loves each of us too much to even think about discarding us. In the resurrection, we see that God is already mending fragile things like you and me. The result is breathtakingly beautiful: a resurrection-shaped life.

CHAPTER ONE

GROWING BEYOND OUR PAST

I didn't intend to start thinking about God,
it just happened.

— Mary Oliver, "Drifting"

D espite the heat and humidity of late-July Florida, I strapped on my shoes for an afternoon run. The relief of getting out of the house and capturing a few quiet minutes on my own outweighed the threat of heat stroke.

Andrew, our firstborn, was just a few weeks old. My wife, Joy, had taken maternity leave from her public-radio job, and since I was on a college faculty, my summer months were my own to structure. So we both spent the first days of Andrew's life sharing his every gassy smile, dirty diaper, and middle-of-the-night feeding. A combination of sleep deprivation and cabin fever was tipping each of us toward new-baby psychosis. So when Joy said, "Jake, I think you need to get out the house. For all our sakes," I jumped at it.

At about the half-mile mark, I'm sure I looked a fright. My heart rate and breathing had evened out, but my face was flushed and sweat had saturated my t-shirt and shorts. One of my older neighbors was shuffling toward his mailbox. As I ran by, he said, "What on earth are you doing?"

I responded, "I'm running from my past."

Pretty clever, right? It seemed funny at the moment. But the phrase kept turning around in my mind. I'm running from my past. Am I running from my past? What am I running from?

At the time, I was just at the beginning of my professional career, straining to establish myself as an expert in an academic field. New parenthood was stretching not only my sense of self but also who Joy and I were to each other as friends and lovers. Challenges of the heart and professional growth were exactly what I had signed up for. My days were rewarding and the future looked promising. Well, mostly. As I was coming to the end of my run, another truth emerged with wrenching clarity. Some of the defining memories of my life were breaking my heart, disrupting my relationships, and dragging me into bouts of shame and sorrow. I couldn't just leave those experiences behind; I was going to have to grow beyond them.

Up to this point I had spent my life pushing ahead, as if a new life as husband, father, and philosophy professor would in time diminish the power of these painful memories. Maybe I could just start over and escape all those old wounds. But now I was beginning to admit that simply moving on was out of the question. After all, unless injury or disease destroyed my memory, my past was going to follow me wherever I went.

Actually, the past doesn't just follow us around. It's a crucial part of our identity. Just ask some people to tell you who they are. I mean, who they *really* are. Once they get beyond telling you that they're a doctor or a lawyer or a machinist, stories about kids or grandkids often follow. Dig a little deeper and they'll start telling you personal stories. They will share their memories with you. They will piece together their past in a way that makes sense to them and that they hope will be acceptable to somebody else.

On a résumé, we can cherry-pick the flattering bits of our experience. We're out to make an impression, to land a job. Nobody lists their biggest flops or most embarrassing missteps. We omit the messy parts of our lives. Coming to terms with our past does not resemble résumé building. We have to be honest with ourselves about everything. Especially the stuff that can still shatter us, enrage us, flatten us, and make us wince. Like those of many faith traditions, Christians have realized this for eons. And we know that processing our memories is most effective when we do it with another. For us, coming to terms with our past is done best with Christ.

Jesus-followers usually call this repentance. And I'm going to use that word too. But before I do, I want to help us recover a depth and breadth of the spiritual practice that Jesus had in mind. Like many of my fellow Christians, I once assumed that repentance focused narrowly on sins. The process went something like this: Admit that you've gone the wrong way, stop where you are, turn around, and get back on the right road. God blots out what you've done in the past and grants you a sort of do-over. God won't hold your past against you.

I've confessed some real doozies. Before taking the run that day, I had received absolution for things done and things left undone more times than I can count. As advertised, confession brought relief from my feelings of guilt. But remorse about my past wasn't the defining problem; I was wounded by my past. I was wounded by abuse, neglect, and exploitation. I needed to find a way to die to the person whose life was shaped by this pain and sorrow in order for a new self to emerge from them.

The Night My Father Killed Me

Like most of us, my soul was bruised by countless things. But one childhood experience crystallizes the woundedness that was finally over-taking me. When I was ten years old, my father, my mother, and I lived in a newly constructed house on the outskirts of a tiny south Georgia town. My maternal grandparents had provided the money to purchase land and to make a down payment for construction. My parents had alternated between periods of living together in low-level combat and taking up separate addresses. When my mother asked my grandparents to loan them the money, I wasn't surprised to hear them quietly ask in their native German, "Are you sure this is going to work out?"

We had moved into the 900-square-foot house a few weeks earlier. Like my mother, I believed that this new setting could give us a new start as a family. My unpredictably angry, violent father would become reliably kind. We could be what I took to be a normal family. Sitting in my room, I heard my father's angry voice echo down the hallway from the den. I hustled down the hall toward a clearly escalating conflict. When I walked through the door, I found my father aiming a pistol at my mother's head. Without thinking I stepped between my parents, putting myself between the gun and my mother. The barrel was now leveled at me.

I said with a calm I still can't account for, "Don't shoot my mother. If you kill her, you'll go to prison. You'll leave me an orphan."

With a sneer, my father glared at me and said, "You'd be better off an orphan."

I stood my ground.

Exactly what happened to break the tension escapes me now. I remember only that my father ended up in my parents' bedroom. My mother and I holed up in my room with the door locked. After what seemed like hours, my mother slipped into the hall and peeked briefly into their room. She ran back and locked the door again. My father was lying on the bed with a shotgun resting on his chest, the barrel tucked under his chin.

In retrospect, I realize that this was a clumsily choreographed production. My father's intent, I now suppose, was to divert our fear and outrage into pity for him; in reality, the whole horror show was a display of manipulation and control. But neither my mother nor my ten-year-old self realized this at the time. We just panicked. The calm I had managed to show earlier in the night was steadily dissolving. When my father crashed through the locked door, whatever composure I had left abandoned me. I hid behind my curtain quaking and sobbing.

This time, my mother ran to protect and comfort me. This wasn't what my father had had in mind. It threw him off his game. So, unbelievably, he switched in an instant from menacing assailant to his version of comforting parent. He assured me that everything was fine. I was overreacting.

My father did not pull the trigger that night. Soon after this episode, my mother left him and—along with me—escaped that little town once and for all. Only we didn't escape entirely; something inside me shattered that night. My father killed a version of me, the version that still hoped that I could be lovable by simply being me. And that murdered ten-year-old me was still running along with me as an adult. Waiting for resurrection. Yearning for new life.

Repentance and Resurrection

What I've come to believe is that repentance is precisely what I needed and what I still need. I needed to learn, however, that repentance is more than a sin-canceling transaction. When we repent, we admit that the sorrows, the losses, the wounds, the betrayals, and the regrets of our past have made us into someone we don't want to be anymore. We die to that self and entrust ourselves to Jesus. From those shattered places in our lives, Christ brings new life; to put it another way: repentance is the beginning of our resurrection. Right here on planet Earth.

Look at the story about Jesus's call of the first disciples. Jesus was strolling along the shore. He saw two sets of fishermen: Peter and Andrew, James and John. Jesus invited them to follow him with the odd promise to transform them from fishermen into fishers of people (Mark 1:16-20). The ordinary life they already knew would provide the root from which eternal life would grow. Repentance does not mean for us—nor did it for them—that we cut ourselves off from our past. All that we've ever done, all that's been done to us, no longer merely defines us and limits us. Our past will become that beyond which we have grown. Even the most harrowing, humbling, and cringe-worthy moments of our lives provide the soil from which Jesus nurtures us into eternal life. If we hand the life shaped by our past over to Jesus, eternal life will emerge from the depths of our day-to-day lives.

Jesus's first sermon pointed us in this direction. The Gospels record the heart of it: "Repent, for the kingdom of heaven has come near" (Matthew 4:17). Some Jesus-followers hear something like this: Repent or else. God's harsh judgment is just around the bend. Time is short. Jesus comes into the picture to get us off the hook for sin. The bad stuff we've done won't count against us as long as we believe that he took the punishment we deserve. In other words, Jesus's message is only about sin and the forgiveness of sin. As long as we conceive of salvation as a rescue operation from the consequences of sin, we will continue to hear "repent" as a requirement for escaping eternal punishment.

But a different message emerges when we reconsider what Jesus means when he says, "The kingdom of heaven has come near." In Jesus himself, the divine has come near. Heaven has reached into our ordinary, everyday lives. The holy is braiding itself into the mundane before we lift a finger. God has initiated a relationship with us prior to even the feeblest moral reflection on our part. Repentance is our response to God's intimate presence in our lives. Flipping Jesus's word order and amplifying the translation will help convey what I mean: "God is breathtakingly close. Open your eyes. Open your heart. Letting God in will really change things for you. Starting with you." The Greek word we frequently translate as "repentance" means a change of heart. Paradoxically, we become ourselves by being changed. Changed by an increasing nearness to God in Christ.

Repentance is the admission that we need to learn how to live; a change of heart, however, happens gradually. We have to grow into it. God's transforming love seeps into our lives sometimes gently, sometimes startlingly, but never all at once. As Ezekiel puts it, God is replacing our heart of stone with a throbbing heart of flesh (Ezekiel 36:26). God replaces the life we made—with our past experiences and our own willpower—with a life grown from divine love. Mortal life with eternal life. The resurrection is shaping our lives even now, but this is not an instantaneous switch.

Learning How to Live

First-century Jewish disciples learned by imitating their rabbis. Following a rabbi did not resemble sitting at a desk, taking notes, and passing exams about the Torah or the Hebrew Bible; disciples devoted themselves to learning how to live a God-shaped life. One learned how to live a life like this by staying close to wise and holy rabbis and by copying their patterns of acting and talking in surprisingly minute detail.

How does the rabbi wash hands? Which sandal does the rabbi put on first? Does the rabbi travel on the Sabbath? If so, how far and by what means? I once heard that some disciples hid in the rabbi's bedroom to learn the proper expression of marital intimacy. Others peeked into the rabbi's bathroom to learn . . . well, these stories may not be true, but they make the point.

Studying Torah is learning how to live a God-shaped life, and disciples got the hang of how to live such a life by emulating their rabbi. Rabbis certainly taught Torah by discussing it, but most important, they imparted Torah to the next generation by embodying it through their everyday actions, common words, and habitual demeanor.

When Peter, James, John, and the rest of the Twelve accepted Jesus's invitation to follow him, they were committing themselves to patterning their lives on Jesus. Like beginning violin students, the disciples hit some sour notes early on. Initially, they may have thought that Jesus was passing on to them his superior grasp of the moral law and the proper spiritual practices. Gradually, they came to realize that they were letting go of the lives they had known in order to receive a new kind of life that Jesus was passing on to them: his very life. Eternal life. Following Jesus is an ongoing pattern of repentance and resurrection, letting go of our own lives so that Jesus can remake them.

Struggling to follow Jesus's example doesn't make the disciples—or any of us—failures or underachievers. On the contrary, mistakes and missteps are part of what it means to follow Jesus to a resurrection-shaped life. I think that may be why Matthew (14:22-33) tells the familiar story of Peter's attempt to walk on water. In the accounts of Matthew, Mark (6:45-52), and John (6:16-21), the disciples have gone ahead of Jesus in a boat. The weather gets rough. In the predawn hours, the disciples spot Jesus strolling across the lake. If we stop with the accounts of Mark and John, the passages tell us only that Jesus is divine. That's an important message, and Matthew conveys it as well. But Matthew adds the bit about Peter getting out of the boat. And it's important to ask why he included it. Scholars have concluded that Matthew had a source that Mark lacked. But that still doesn't explain why Matthew thought it important to include the Peter episode in the larger story he was telling. My hunch is that he wanted to show us what discipleship meant in light of what we had just learned about Jesus's identity.

Jesus is God incarnate. So, imitating Jesus is an impossibly high goal for ordinary slobs like us. It's like asking somebody to defy the laws of gravity. And, of course, that's just what Jesus does. He urges us to walk on water.

Crucially, he also knows what that will mean for us. Let's look more closely at the passage.

Peter essentially says to Jesus, "If that's you, tell me to come out there with you." Peter climbs over the gunwale, takes a few steps, and then sinks. Jesus grabs him and hauls him into the boat. He says, "You of little faith, why did you doubt?" (Matthew 14:31).

You've probably heard lots of sermons about Peter's faith deficit. Me too. If he had only believed strenuously enough, preachers have said, he would never have sunk. Frequently, we're harangued about our own puny faith and told to buck up. Believe harder!

Well, baloney!

For starters, remember that Peter was a disciple. He took the risk of imitating Jesus doing impossible things. It's what he had signed up for. Besides, Peter had already come to expect Jesus to do and say unthinkable things:

- Turn the other cheek. Don't imagine that violence will solve anything.
- Forgive the unrepentant. Repeatedly. How you feel about it isn't the point.
- Love your enemy. Even the dangerous one who hates your guts.
- Give your stuff away because someone else needs it. Don't even ask about who deserves it.
- See everybody—simply everybody—as infinitely valuable. Nobody is here to serve your agenda, gratify your desires, or live up to your expectations.
- Eat with sinners. Befriend outcasts. Get over yourself.

This is what a resurrection-shaped life looks like on this planet. We can't get there on our own. Jesus imparts a life like that to us, but we also have spiritual work to do. We have to relinquish our habits of coercion and violence to turn the other cheek. Forgiving doesn't happen while we insist on payback. When we repent, we die to our old self so that Jesus can raise us to a new kind of life.

Jesus is showing us what it means to live, to have eternal life. Eternal life is loving in a way that resembles God. And, yes, while our street address is on planet Earth, this will be like walking on water. Impossible! We will sink. And sinking is where the growth happens. Once we've been brought back to the safety of the boat, will we step back out on the waves again?

I imagine that when Jesus welcomed Peter out on the waves, he knew that Peter would sink. Who wouldn't? Jesus wasn't testing Peter, waiting to see how tenaciously he would cling to his beliefs. In fact, getting out of the boat was Peter's idea. Jesus merely encouraged him. It's as if Jesus said, "Go for it! Live a little!" When Jesus pulled Peter back into the boat, he said, "You of little faith, why did you doubt?" I for one do not hear a scolding tone. Instead, I hear something like compassion and encouragement. Jesus recognized that Peter had room to grow; nobody gets the hang of living like Jesus all at once. Jesus teaches us to do things that most ordinary people call naive or just plain crazy. Anybody is going to be at least a little hesitant at first. In a word, the resurrection shapes us gradually. We grow into eternal life one step at a time. In a way, it's like immigrating to a whole new world.

Immigrating to the New World

For my birthday, Joy surprised me with a framed photograph of my twenty-year-old mother, Trudy. Someone had taken the photo aboard the ship that brought her to America. Doing some genealogical work while we were visiting Salt Lake City, Joy came across that photograph and the passenger manifest of *Vulcania*.

Traveling completely alone, my mother took the seventeen-hour train trip from Linz, Austria, to the port in Genoa, Italy. There she boarded *Vulcania* for a roughly three-week ocean crossing. Trudy's possessions fit into a single flimsy suitcase. She arrived at Ellis Island on October 29, 1949.

The word *cruise* suggests luxury. This trip was anything but that. The ship's manifest lists my mother among those in alien tourist class. Read that as "steerage." The photo captures her dining among dozens of other passengers in an unadorned, cramped compartment more suitable to storing cargo than hosting people. The simple tables and the small chairs reminded me of lunchrooms from my middle school days. Plainly dressed diners sit elbow to elbow with their backs nearly touching the people at the table behind them. My mother sits in the background. Even though people in the foreground may have been the photographer's intended subject, Trudy's determined profile and wavy brunette hair are unmistakable.

When I was twenty, going away to college seemed like a big move. Spring-break trips with friends and study-abroad programs felt like adventures. Traveling all alone to a distant country with no job, no facility with the language, and no local support system would have been out of the question for me. Then again, I had not survived daily Allied bombing and internment in a Nazi concentration camp. These experiences had forged my mother into sterner stuff than I was at the same age.

War's indiscriminate slaughter and the Nazi state's systematic violence against what it viewed as undesirable elements had bruised and battered Trudy's soul and body. And yet she emerged from those experiences with a childlike humor, a tender acceptance of others' quirks and idiosyncrasies, and an ability to make even simple moments into a party. We would watch cartoons together and laugh out loud at episodes of *The Little Rascals*. During my teen and young adult years, her insistence that other people were doing the best they could simply drove me crazy. By contrast, I did appreciate her ability to find reason to celebrate with sweets at the least provocation.

You might think that my mother was escaping the rubble of bombed-out Austria and fleeing the Soviet threat poised just across the Danube in her then-occupied hometown of Linz. And such thoughts must surely have played some part in her decision to make such a risky journey. But I believe that it would be more accurate to say that my mother was inspired. Inspired by a dream of greater life. When Trudy talked about immigrating to America, she never talked about getting rich or famous. She talked about being free.

As I look back on it, I realize that my mother wasn't talking about civil rights as such. She was getting at something deeper and more abiding. In America, she perceived a New World, a world redolent with the promise that she—and everyone in it—could become a fully human person. I believe that my mother was swept along by a dream and a longing analogous to what the disciples experienced when the newly risen Jesus appeared to them.

Here's how the Gospel writer John described that experience (John 20:19-29). The disciples were huddled in a locked room, hiding for fear of violence. Jesus appeared, and commissioned them to go into the world. Then, he breathed on them. The breathing thing seems a little weird, but it's crucial. Jesus, you see, inspired them. They were moved not by the force of a command but by the excitement of inspiration. Consider the word *inspire*. Its roots mean to breathe in, to fill with breath. Remember that God brought a heap of dust to life by breathing into it. The Book of Genesis calls that dust-person Adam.

Jesus breathed new life into his disciples. His resurrection animated them with the dream of a New World, a world where love dissolves hatred. Where compassion displaces fear of strangers. Where generosity eliminates deprivation and respect guards the dignity of all. This is, of course, not the world we inhabit—at least not yet. And that is why Jesus sent them. He didn't tell them to wait around until he waved a magic wand. He inspired them to take the risky journey from the Old World they still inhabited toward the New World they longed for.

That journey involves immense risk. Jesus puts it this way. "If you forgive the sins of any, they are forgiven them; if you retain the sins of any, they are retained" (John 20:23). In other words, the peace and reconciliation we dream of starts with us. It's God's dream, all right. We can't get there without God. But God will only make this New World a reality through us. We will get to a mended world only by stepping out toward it ourselves, even in the midst of the pain and sorrow and violence that makes headlines every day. If we don't forgive, forgiveness won't happen. If we don't seek reconciliation, reconciliation will never exist. If we wait for others to be ready for forgiveness or until it's safe to offer reconciliation, they will never come to pass. In the crucifixion, Jesus himself showed us that getting to the New World is not for sissies. And yet, the promise of his resurrection is that our risks—though costly—will not be in vain.

My mother was not a theologian; she was an immigrant. An immigrant inspired to set sail for a new world. Strictly speaking, that's what Jesus is inspiring us to do when he invites us to repent: to leave an old world, an old life, behind and to set sail for a resurrection-shaped world. The first leg of that journey is our own resurrection-shaped life.

REFLECTION QUESTIONS

1. What idea, image, story, or passage from this chapter grabbed your attention or captured your imagination? How did it affirm, challenge, conflict with, or expand how you've been thinking about repentance?

2. The author broadens the definition of repentance, saying that in repentance we grow beyond not only past sins but also regrets, wounds, and losses. Explore this amplified idea of repentance.

3. The author explains that to repent means to change your heart or mind. What does he mean by this? Have you experienced a change of heart or mind in this way? Or are you struggling with a change of heart or mind now?

4. Have you ever struggled with things in your past? How have you grown beyond wounds or feelings of remorse or losses?

5. Are any old memories, regrets, or resentments affecting how you see yourself, relate to other people, or feel about God? What might help lead you to a change of heart and a new life?

CHAPTER TWO

The Meaning of Suffering

And then I remembered this basic religious principle
that God isn't there to take away our suffering or our pain
but to fill it with his or her presence.

—Anne Lamott, *Traveling Mercies*

My stomach was churning. Joy and I had paid our entrance fee to the United States Holocaust Memorial Museum in Washington, DC. We were approaching the rack that held hundreds of small cards bearing a photo and a brief bio of a person interred in one of the Nazi concentration camps. I selected a card. With guilty relief I saw that the card I had chosen did not display my mother's face.

My mother, Trudy—Edeltraud, before Ellis Island officials Americanized her name—grew up in Linz, Austria. Like the vast majority of Austrians, she was Roman Catholic. She was a bit of a handful for her parents, but not politically involved. She was known to ditch school to go sledding. As my mom told it, she would hike up her skirt and slide down a local hill on her bloomers. Around her fifteenth birthday, the Nazis sent Trudy to Mauthausen.

My mother never told me why the Gestapo arrested her and sent her to a concentration camp. She was not Jewish or Roma, so she was not a usual target for the Final Solution. Long after my mother's death, I finally went looking for answers.

I discovered that the Germans had classified Mauthausen's juvenile inmates into categories. Nearly six thousand were foreign civilian laborers, followed by five thousand political prisoners, then almost four thousand Jews. None of these groupings described my mother. By process of elimination, only one category remained within which she might have been placed: antisocial element. My mother was one of twenty young people sentenced to death by forced labor for being an antisocial element.

There were no gas chambers or ovens at Mauthausen. Instead, the camp used crushingly strenuous labor and relentlessly long hours to exterminate prisoners. Fed starvation rations and housed in filthy, cramped, and drafty quarters, inmates gradually succumbed to exhaustion and disease. From the cruel perspective of the Nazis, Mauthausen represented a win-win. German industry profited from slave labor, and the Third Reich accomplished the mass execution of undesirables. Initially, the Nazis filled the camp with adults. Eventually, they added a juvenile section to the camp. The number of juvenile inmates began to rise dramatically in 1944, reaching 78,000 by March 1945.

The camp was never a topic of conversation in our home. We had an old, coarsely woven blanket in a closet. I asked once why we kept a tattered, scratchy thing like that. We never used it. My mother said something like, "It came from Mauthausen. That was a Nazi camp near Linz. They sent me there." At a later point, she told me glowingly about her liberation. American soldiers found her unconscious, severely beaten, and left for dead. But she told me nothing further.

The horrors of the camp first became a graphic reality for me in high school from other sources. We watched the French documentary *Night and Fog*.[1] In grainy black-and-white images, British liberators piled emaciated corpses like cordwood at Auschwitz-Birkenau. Bulldozers shoved mounds of those corpses into mass graves. They discovered warehouses that stored the victims' hair, clothing, and spectacles in ghastly heaps. The Nazis repurposed everything for the Reich. Then a religion teacher assigned Viktor Frankl's *Man's Search for Meaning*.[2] As a teenager, I was riveted by his harrowing experiences in Auschwitz and then Dachau. Years later, I would come to appreciate his psychological theories.

By the time Joy and I visited the Holocaust Museum, I thought I was well-schooled in the facts about the Nazi genocide. But as I moved slowly through the photos and the news clips, the exhibits re-creating camp life and the survivors' stories, the sorrow I had felt for so long about the Holocaust, and about my mother's experiences specifically, began gradually to give rise to the question about suffering that occupies this chapter. Can we find meaning in the world's suffering?

Questions About Suffering

It's not as if I had never thought deeply about suffering before touring the Holocaust Museum. On the contrary, in my former life teaching philosophy to college students, I routinely included a section on the problem of evil in my introductory courses. But in those classes, we were asking a different question. For centuries, theologians and philosophers have asked, "How could a loving, all-good, all-powerful, and all-knowing God allow human misery?" I explored with my students how to square belief in a loving God—or any God at all—with a world filled with heartache, deprivation, and pain. The Holocaust served as an especially effective intellectual challenge to the concept of God that many of us had inherited. Some of my students were actively wrestling with the faith they had been brought up with. Others had already discarded the religion of their parents. A few were even antagonistic toward belief in God in any form. In short, the questions we were asking were these: Can we find an argument that justifies our belief in God despite the existence of human suffering? And, given the fact of human suffering, what must God be like?

Some students solved the problem for themselves by placing the blame entirely on human shoulders. They saw no reason to change their concept of God. Others revised their thoughts about the divine. They reasoned that God's hands were tied. To give humans freedom to make choices, God could not take away our ability to choose evil. So, God probably isn't all-powerful. For that matter, since we're free, God can't foresee with certainty what we will do next. No one can know what people will do until they've actually done it. So, for them, God could not be all-knowing. As you might imagine, those who had already dismissed the idea of God found confirmation for their disbelief in the assigned readings and class discussions.

Sharpening our minds with intellectual work is immensely valuable. But as the years of teaching the traditional philosophical approach to the problem of evil went by, I grew increasingly dissatisfied with where this purely conceptual work could take me. The arguments remained as logically persuasive or as flawed as they had always been, but I had a sense that I was failing to get at the real issue—the living truth—waiting to be found in the depths of human suffering. It was no longer enough for me to find a way to get God off the hook for the pain and the fear and the sorrow of the world. I wanted to experience and to connect with a God for whom human suffering matters. And I yearned to have a felt sense that this God is doing something about the world's suffering. I needed a new question to guide my reflections.

Everything I had learned about the Holocaust had been nudging me toward a new approach to suffering. And the tipping point came when I read how the camp's Nazi bureaucrats classified my mother: "anti-social element." I read that to mean "miscellaneous." In other words, the Nazis had no real reason to sentence her to a slow, agonizing death. There was no plan—not even an evil, genocidal plan like the Final Solution—that could account for her misery. She was just in the wrong place at the wrong time. This realization shattered me with overpowering compassion. And my compassion quickly broadened from empathy for my mother to empathy for all those who suffer. I realized that many will wonder if their agony—and by extension the life that has led up to it—has any meaning at all. Is this horrible moment all that life will come to? From the cross even Jesus cried, "My God, my God, why have you forsaken me?" (Matthew 27:46).

The guiding question that I arrived at—and the question at the heart of this chapter—is this: How will God make the world's suffering mean something? If we see in the cross God's embrace of the world's suffering, we will see in the risen Christ God's response to that suffering. The empty tomb assures us that, in Christ, suffering and death can lead to new life. For instance, my mother emerged from the deprivations and suffering of the death camps with two related marks of a resurrection-shaped life. First, she embraced life with an inextinguishable sense of hope. Her oft-repeated mantra was: Tomorrow is another a day. Additionally, she embodied a compassion that made her frightfully vulnerable to the suffering and the sorrows of others. My teenaged self had little patience or respect for my mother's dogged hopefulness and her empathy with society's castoffs and the down-on-their-luck. Nevertheless I see that, despite my resistance and self-absorption, my mother imparted this way of living to me. Admittedly, my mom never spoke of her life in the theological terms that I am using here. And yet, I see in her way of living the shape of resurrection in ordinary life. She gave me my first lessons in a paradoxical truth. By God's grace, a new life—what I'm calling a resurrection-shaped life—emerges from suffering and sorrow. One way in which that new life emerges is in our unguarded engagement with the suffering of others.

Suffering with Others

In sacramental churches, baptism is more than a mere re-enactment of death and resurrection. Baptism is participation in the mystery of rising from death to new life. Author Sara Miles once said, "Choosing to get pregnant in a war is the closest experience I've had to . . . getting baptized." In her wartime pregnancy, Miles began a journey into suffering and love whose redemptive meaning cracked open in her baptism. Unique as it is in its details, her story is the story of all the baptized.[3] And it's a window on what it means to inhabit a resurrection-shaped life.

Miles got pregnant in the fall of 1988 while she was covering the civil war in El Salvador as a reporter. It was a brutal conflict. As she recalls, "Every morning during that fall of 1988 I'd . . . learn that a body had been dumped in the ravine [at the end of my street]."[4] Death squads descended on men, women, and children. Military and guerrilla forces sprayed each other with bullets on public streets heedless of civilians in the line of fire. This was not a safe place—or even a sane place—to be carrying a baby, especially for someone who could simply fly back to the United States. And yet, she was swept away by a longing for new life.

Before her pregnancy, Miles had reported other people's suffering.

But she had remained at a safe, journalistic distance. Now that she was carrying a child in her own womb, suffering had become personal. She wrote, "I saw hungry kids, maimed kids, lost kids, scared kids, sick kids, shot kids. . . . Night after night, I knew mothers and fathers were still awake, waiting for their children to come home alive. I was heading straight into that suffering, as well as into love."[5] Miles felt in her own body what every parent I know can tell you. When your child hurts, your own heart breaks. Parents are forever vulnerable to the world through their daughters and sons. And Miles's own tender vulnerability gave her a visceral feeling of solidarity with the sufferings of all those parents and children around her. Baptism would provide the crucial redemptive element to the wartime lessons of suffering and love. Suffering for others can lead to new life.

Miles came to faith as a forty-something, around a decade after becoming a mother. She chose to be baptized. Or more accurately, a longing for new life drew her to the font. This was especially baffling for her, her friends, and her family. None in her circle had a religious bone in his or her body. Her parents had raised her as a secularist. Over the years, she had found no reason to think of religious beliefs as anything more than superstition. For no apparent reason, she had wandered into St. Gregory of Nyssa Episcopal Church. Having not the slightest clue about what was going on, she stumbled her way through the liturgy and received communion.

When she took the bread and wine into her mouth, she knew instantly that Jesus had entered into her, that this Jesus character is real and really conveys himself to us in those humble elements. Well, strictly speaking, this experience did not compute for her at the time. What she tasted and felt clashed with everything that she understood to be true. In time, and with considerable intellectual and emotional wrestling, she yielded to her desire for new life. She got baptized. And this is what her baptism revealed: "Sometimes I felt so uplifted by the thought of being special, marked as Christ's own, that I forgot baptism wasn't about me. And it wasn't about the event, the particular day the water would wet me. . . . I was baptized . . . into the crucifixion of the world. And into living, daily redemption."[6]

Like Miles, we are all baptized into solidarity with each other's suffering and hunger for new life. And we are baptized into Jesus. Jesus embraces and redeems the world's suffering through our hands and feet. In an interview, Miles put it this way:

> For me, it's about actually doing the work that Jesus gives his disciples: feeding, healing, touching the ritually unclean, forgiving, raising the dead. And entering into this work, following Jesus, allows us to believe what seems, on the face of it, ridiculous: that God has faith in us. That God trusts us—people no better or smarter or more faithful than the cowardly housewives and fishermen he chose as his disciples—to bear God in our bodies and do God's work in the world.[7]

We are the Body of Christ. We "bear God in our bodies." Jesus loves through us to heal and renew our scarred and weary world. The redemptive power of suffering and love helps us understand why Jesus teaches us to turn the other cheek (Matthew 5:39). Our first impulse is to avoid pain and to do what it takes to survive. News reports and history books are filled with a common human story. We habitually depend upon the threat of violence to prevent others from hurting us. When someone injures us or insults us, our animal impulse is to strike back, to hurt our attacker worse. We seek to bruise and to intimidate our opponents into fearful submission. In other words, we seek to minimize our own suffering, even if it comes at the expense of someone else's misery.

Jesus is very clear. This way of walking the planet will leave the world wounded and disfigured. Instead, Jesus teaches us to take up our cross and follow him. Only love—in all its vulnerability to the suffering of others and all its risk of injury to ourselves—will heal and transfigure the world. So, when Jesus says, "Do not resist an evildoer," he is not advocating passive submission to cruelty and abuse, oppression and deprivation (Matthew 5:39). Instead, Jesus wants us to resist evil without becoming evil ourselves.

My friend Bishop Nick Knisely of Rhode Island shared a helpful example of this Christian response to evil and violence when he addressed dealing with nastiness on social media: The solution to pollution is dilution. Don't respond to nasty tweets or inflammatory Facebook posts in kind. Flood social media with truth and kindness and generosity. Likewise, instead of trying to crush evil, overwhelm evil with good. Feed the hungry. Help addicts get sober. Teach job skills. Share your support network with those who are falling through the cracks. Befriend the bullied. Do none of this in condescension, but in solidarity.

Don't withhold yourself for fear of injury to body or soul. Do the good that's right in front of you. Every day. Our own small acts of compassion and decency might not seem like much in this big, dangerous, aching world. But together, the billions of hands and feet shaped by the resurrection are a mighty force. Resurrection happens through us. We must be patiently relentless. Jesus will not wave a magic wand or flip a new-creation switch. A resurrection-shaped world does not happen in an instant or take place automatically. Resurrection-shaped life for this world is a centuries-long rising tide. From time to time it seems to recede. But eventually, the suffering love of Jesus will cleanse this world of hate and cruelty, degradation and persecution. And in Christ a renewed world will rise through frail and fragile hands like ours. Paradoxically, we discover meaning in our lives when we suffer for a higher purpose.

Suffering for a Higher Purpose

Like lots of adolescent boys, I dreamed alternately of being an Olympic athlete or a rock star. I imagined leaning into the tape at the finish line or laying down riffs in a packed auditorium. Not a single one of these fantasies included hours upon hours of grueling, repetitive workouts on the track and at the gym; images of sitting alone with my guitar practicing scales until my fingers bled never even occurred to me. Obviously, no Olympic team sought me out. And Bruce Springsteen I'm not. Even if I had possessed the raw talent to run the 100 meters at an international level or to cut records for a major label, one thing was missing—or should I say, ten thousand things were missing.

In his book *Outliers*, Malcolm Gladwell says that to master an art or a craft takes ten thousand hours of practice.[8] If you want to take on Usain Bolt in Tokyo, then you'll be spending the equivalent of about 420 uninterrupted, sleepless days worth of pounding the track and pumping iron. And to accumulate those ten thousand hours, you'll probably miss spring-break trips to the beach with your buddies, midnight movie premiers, and spontaneous road trips. We hear all the time that we should pursue our dreams, as if the dream itself will motivate us. But as author Mark Manson points out, a dream becomes a genuinely motivating force in our lives when we commit to the suffering involved in realizing that dream.[9] Manson's insight leads us back to this chapter's opening question. Can we find meaning in the world's suffering? Manson helps us see that suffering becomes meaningful when it is endured for the sake of the higher purpose to which our lives are devoted. And crucially, pursuing a higher purpose will always involve suffering.

Manson is not a Christian. Nevertheless, his perspective helps us understand the suffering of Jesus and the meaning of suffering in our own lives as followers of Christ. And what he says contrasts sharply with what many of us take to be common sense. We are a pain-avoidant culture. For instance, the shelves at your local pharmacy or grocery are usually cluttered with Tylenol, Advil, Aleve, and the like. "Suffering," the over-the-counter aisle suggests, "is for losers." Our aversion to suffering has infected Christianity. A host of smiling, successful preachers insist that our faith will summon material wealth and bodily health down from the heavens. Believe, and feel the lumbago vanish. This is a peculiar message from a faith tradition whose defining symbol is a cross.

As Manson points out, suffering is a part of life. You can try to avoid it all you like. Plenty of people do. But suffer we will. Ironically, some of the people who pursue a pain-free existence most obsessively end up suffering most tragically. Addicts and alcoholics initially find escape from the sorrows and hardships of this life in their substance of choice—just look at the staggering increase in opioid addiction. But eventually, the compulsion for the next fix or the next drink can cost them family, career, friends, and health of body and mind.

We will suffer. However, our suffering can be a crucial dimension of a deeply meaningful life. We can choose. We can choose what dream we are willing to suffer for. And that dream infuses the suffering with meaning. Take, for example, the story of Jonathan Myrick Daniels.

In March of 1965, Martin Luther King Jr. sent out a call to students and clergy. He urged them to join him in a march from Selma, Alabama, to the state capitol in Montgomery. Jonathan Myrick Daniels was a twenty-six-year-old seminarian at the Episcopal Theological School in Cambridge, Massachusetts. Along with several of his fellow students, Daniels received permission to miss classes in order to participate in the now-famous march.

His intention was to return to Cambridge at the end of the weekend; however, he and his friend Judith Upham missed the return bus. Apparently, this delay gave them time to realize that they were needed in the civil rights movement. The seminary administration granted them permission to stay in Alabama and complete their semester's work independently.

The Wests, a local African American family, gave Daniels a place to stay while he continued his civil rights work into the summer. In August, Daniels participated in picketing whites-only stores in Fort Deposit, Alabama. Along with nearly thirty others, he was arrested and jailed in nearby Hayneville. After a long delay, the prisoners were released with no transportation back to Fort Deposit.

As the group waited for their ride, Daniels, a Catholic priest, and two black women strolled to the only store in town that served people of color.

As they arrived at Varner's Cash Store, they saw a white man barring the door. He held a shotgun and had a pistol strapped to his hip.

As the four activists approached, the man, Tom Coleman, aimed the shotgun at seventeen-year-old Ruby Sales. Daniels pushed her aside as Coleman opened fire, taking the shotgun's full load and dying instantly. Coleman claimed self-defense. An all-white jury acquitted him.

Jonathan Daniels did not go to the South to spend hot summer days jammed into an overcrowded jail cell that had no air-conditioning and reeked from overflowing toilets. And he certainly had no intention of dying on a dusty street in the middle of nowhere. But he understood that all this might happen. His experiences in the South had provided for him a kind of clarity. He was willing to make these sacrifices for the higher purpose of justice and human dignity.

When we devote ourselves to a higher purpose, we set aside dreams for which we are unwilling to suffer. That's what Daniels did. And that is what Jesus was doing in his confrontation with Satan in the wilderness (Matthew 4:1-11).

"Turn these stones into a bag of nice hot bagels," Satan says. Jesus declines. Filling your own belly is good; it relieves your physical discomfort. But it won't add significance to the wounds and sorrows that litter even the most charmed life.

"Toss yourself from the steeple. If you're as holy as you think you are, God will catch you before you hit the pavement." Again, Jesus declines. A life shaped by spiritual disciplines is a good thing. But trying to impress others—even God—with how regularly and fervently you pray misses the point. Suffering just to prove how holy you are doesn't sound all that holy.

"OK," Satan says, "how about political power and military muscle then? You can whip the world into shape. Make everybody follow the right kind of values." Jesus is blunt this time. A life devoted to making others suffer for the sake of control has nothing to do with God. On the contrary, in Jesus, God comes to us to redeem all suffering.

And with this final temptation, Jesus arrives at his moment of clarity about the higher purpose of his life: Jesus commits himself to the healing of the world. He does whatever it takes to make the world whole. He feeds the hungry, mends the sick, and restores lunatics to sanity. He breaks bread with streetwalkers and extortionists, drug addicts and con artists. By costly example, he teaches us to forgive the unrepentant, to resist the violent with compassionate truth, and to give the thief who steals your shoes the shirt off your own back.

The religious establishment branded Jesus a troublemaker and a heretic. The political powers perceived him as a threat to the status quo and killed him. Jesus suffered and gave his life for the sake of the higher purpose of the world's wholeness. By raising him from the dead, God inscribed Jesus's suffering—and all suffering for the sake of healing the world—with infinite and eternal meaning. God sets things right through this kind of suffering, suffering endured for the sake of love.

We will suffer, we frail and fragile mortals. And yet we can do more than merely endure senseless misery. Jesus challenges us to choose his dream as the higher purpose that guides our lives: to suffer for the healing of the world. To take up the cross and follow him. To follow him through suffering to life eternal.

REFLECTION QUESTIONS

1. What idea, image, story, or passage from this chapter grabbed your attention or captured your imagination? How does it affirm, challenge, conflict with, or expand how you've been thinking about suffering?
2. Has suffering ever made you doubt the existence of God? Where did that doubt lead you in your relationship with God? Do you know others whose belief in God stumbles over the suffering in the world? What would you say to them after reading this chapter?
3. Tell a story about a time that you or someone you love suffered. How did that experience shape your understanding of God? Your understanding of the meaning of suffering?
4. Talk about a time that your compassion for others has brought you suffering. Did you find meaning in that experience? Did it shape your life?
5. The author talks about suffering for a higher purpose. What do you think he means by that? Have you had such an experience?

CHAPTER THREE

RECOVERING FROM SHAME AND BLAME

The people who know God well—mystics, hermits, prayerful people, those who risk everything to find God—always meet a lover, not a dictator.

—Richard Rohr, *Everything Belongs*

At first light, I shuffled into the kitchen to make coffee. A saucepan sat on the stove. As I reached for our old-school Melitta pour-over carafe, I simultaneously jerked the saucepan off the unlit burner. Cold water splashed onto my face and drenched the front of my t-shirt. I blurted out, "Who put water in this pan!"

My shout was an involuntary reaction, like saying *#%! when stubbing your toe or jamming your funny bone. That's not what Joy heard. Responding to my panicked tone, she rushed into the kitchen expecting to find third-degree burns or a grease fire. Instead, she saw me standing in a shallow puddle holding a coffeepot in one hand and a saucepan in the other. Water dripped steadily from my long, scraggly beard to the linoleum at my feet.

She looked at me, confused by the incongruity of the shriek she had heard at a distance and the humorous scene now on display in front of her. Her initial concern gave way first to an amused twinkle in her eye and then to good-natured laughter. After many years of marriage, I now recognize that response. That look and that laugh say something like, "Isn't life funny? And don't we all take ourselves too seriously?" Joy thought she was laughing *with* me. But, at that time, we hadn't been together for very long, so instead of responding to her, I responded from a long-developed habit of shame. I assumed that she was laughing *at* me.

Joy was experiencing one of life's little slapstick-comedy moments. I was feeling humiliated and growing increasingly indignant. As far as I was concerned, somebody had to be at fault for how ridiculous I looked and felt. You see, I'm a blamer. Or, more accurately, I'm a recovering blamer given to occasional relapses.

Feelings of shame lie at the bottom of my faultfinding. The research of psychologists and sociologists like Brené Brown suggest that I am not alone. Brown describes blame as a preconscious strategy for off-loading strong, painful emotions.[1] Shame is a strong and painful feeling of deep unworthiness.[2] It's as if we can't stop hearing a harsh, internal judge repeatedly pronouncing the sentence, "You don't measure up and you never will." I didn't choose to have that voice rattling around in my head. It took up residence, uninvited, at a very early age.

The Voice of Shame

The school year had just ended. Summer stretched out before me for an eternity. At least, that's how it seemed to my ten-year-old self. I was playing with a couple of kids at the end of my old street. I didn't know them well. Their names are lost to me now.

Like most of the houses in my old neighborhood, their home was probably a rental. The front porch sagged in the middle, giving the impression that the whole building was gradually collapsing in on itself. The walls were shedding their battered asbestos shingles in various places. We were playing in the front yard, a sun-hardened patch of red clay dotted with small clumps of untended weeds.

The boys' mother leaned out of a screen door at the side of the house. She looked down at me from the stoop and said, "I thought you built that fancy new house out on the bypass. What's the matter? Couldn't y'all make the payments?" She was smiling in a way that didn't seem friendly.

My throat tightened and my eyes began to water. I looked down at my feet. "Yes, ma'am," I mumbled.

When I glanced up, I noticed that her expression seemed brighter, as if someone had paid her a compliment. "Well, that's just what happens to some people." She said the words with an air of triumph, turned back to the house, and let the screen door slam behind her.

Choking back tears I made some excuse and walked off toward my own apartment. I was living in a shabby, furnished set of rooms in an old house that my mother had rented after leaving my father. You see, my father still lived in that nice, newly built house. Actually, it was the 900-square-foot house I mentioned in chapter 1. My mother had gathered me up with the belongings she could carry and escaped her abuser.

The mother of those boys assumed that I was back in the old neighborhood because we had gotten what was coming to us. We had put on airs by building a house that people like us had no business living in. We had tried to look like we were better than she was, better than the people like her. It did her heart good to see somebody like us put in our place. We were, she supposed, getting a well-deserved taste of shame.

Shame was crushing me, all right. But the woman was utterly wrong about the source of my deep feelings of humiliation. My world wasn't right. And since I was accustomed to finding somebody to blame when things went wrong, I had identified the likeliest candidate: me.

It's not that I thought that I had done something immoral. I was wrong simply by virtue of being me. My speech was garbled by an uncorrected cleft palate—everybody saw me as deformed. People did not say "immigrant" in that small, rural town. My mother was a foreigner. She didn't talk right. Act right. She didn't belong. And, of course, I didn't belong as a result. Now my parents were getting a divorce. In that place and at that time, being divorced made a person less than others. The demise of my parents' marriage tainted me. As I said, I was wrong by virtue of being me.

That is what shame looks and feels like. Shame is different from guilt. Feelings of guilt arise from specific wrongdoing. Something we did—or neglected to do—fell short of the mark. Remorse urges us to seek forgiveness, to make things right, and to amend our ways. By contrast, shame is the visceral sense that we are unlovable. All of us will encounter rejection and even contempt from other people at one time or another. When we're weighed down by shame, we start to believe that we deserve no better. We're just no good and our critics have found us out.

All humans possess inherent dignity and unconditional worth. Each of us deserves respect. And yet, to assert these truths while in the grip of shame rings hollow to our own ears. We can't really believe it because we don't feel it. Overcoming shame involves changing our minds about ourselves. And Jesus came in part to help us do precisely that. Jesus changes our minds about ourselves by changing our minds about God. However, like many people I know, I tried to escape feelings of shame by accumulating accomplishments. I pursued success, mistakenly believing that my achievements would make me into somebody lovable to others and bring peace to my own soul.

Losing Yourself to Be Yourself

I discovered something after spending years chasing achievements. If you spend your life trying to make yourself lovable, you will never feel loved. Let me explain by way of another story.

When I was in high school, one of my favorite teachers, Sister Charleen Klister, taught me to write. In her sophomore English class at St. Pius X, we handed in essays every week. I was not especially disciplined about any of this; I frequently got to school only to remember in a panic that an essay was due that very morning. I would race the day's start bell to churn out the required word count.

Halfway through the school year, Sister Charleen reminded us to turn in our journals—the journals that were supposed to contain our daily reflections for the past several months. The journal that I had been completely blowing off. I devoted an entire weekend to writing journal entries. To my credit, the first entry explained what I was doing. At a few points, all I could think to write was that I couldn't think what to write.

These hurriedly scribbled weekly essays and doggedly recorded journal entries must have been agony to read. But Sister Charleen did read them. And responded to them. In detail. She didn't make corrections in red or mark out harebrained errors. In the margins alongside ideas that energized me, she shared her thoughtful responses. Good turns of phrase caught her eye, and she was generous and instructive with her compliments. The most critical thing she ever wrote was in response to one of the very last of those awful journal entries. She said, "I can tell you're really getting tired now."

Sister Charleen believed in my ability as a writer, and she wanted me to believe in myself. So, as a sign of her confidence in me, she nominated me as one of two students to represent the school in a timed essay competition. My fellow contestant and I were placed in the same room at a shared table. Serving as our proctor, Sister Charleen started the clock, unsealed the envelope containing the secret theme, and handed us each a copy of the chosen topic: What is the American Dream?

I drew a blank. A total zilch.

The guy next to me wrote furiously as soon as he got the question. I sat there staring at a blank page. Spring slowly turned to summer. With each second I got more anxious and hoped more fervently that my fellow writer would succumb to a seizure or lose control of his bladder. As the final gong approached, I started writing a disjointed jumble of lame ideas. At no point did I ever figure out what I was trying to say. I had nothing to write. I just had to write something.

When time was up, Charleen collected our papers. Before mailing our essays off to the judges, she sat with us and read each one. She clearly loved what the other guy had written. Her smile and glittering eyes confirmed for me that he was a jerk and a swine. The sympathetic look on her face as she read my word salad said, "I can tell you were really freaking out here." At the time, I read her expression as disappointment. Years later, I learned that she understood how rotten and defeated I felt. She yearned for me to see things—to see the world and myself—in a different light.

In retrospect, I realize that it was my dread of failure that undid me that day. Failure, even perceived failure, would set loose in me an avalanche of shame. This was especially the case since I had come to believe that achievement was my only pathway to being loved and accepted. No wonder the theme of the competition stumped me. It hooked me in an especially vulnerable place. Like many people, I had equated the American Dream with success. I had interpreted the freedom to pursue happiness as a challenge to transform myself into somebody worthy of respect and affection. If I failed, I wasn't just a loser. I was a contemptible nobody. To make matters worse, I was starting from what I perceived to be a significant deficit. We were working class. My divorced single mother was a grocery cashier who lived with her parents. She and my grandparents were immigrants with sketchy English skills. What I would learn years later is that no level of achievement would free me from the shame that repeatedly threatened to overwhelm me.

Some people dream of becoming billionaires or presidents, rock stars, big-time athletes, or media celebrities. They strive to accumulate the wealth, wield the power, or win the admiration that will finally bring their soul to rest. Until then, life is a ceaseless striving to be something they aren't yet. To arrive. The problem is that they never really arrive so long as they believe that being lovable is something to strive for and achieve:

- Even when you're a billionaire, there's somebody with a few billion more.
- You can't be everybody's favorite president or always draw the biggest crowds, and eventually you'll be out of office anyway.
- All sports records get surpassed.
- Even the most popular television shows are at the mercy of the current season's ratings.

If you spend your life trying to ensure your significance and assure yourself of your own worth through your accomplishments, the feeling of self-worth will always elude you. You will become addicted to striving, fear being found out as a fraud, resent being unappreciated, and continue to strike out at others to soothe your own misery. I think Jesus was getting at something like this when he said, "Blessed are the poor in spirit" (Matthew 5:3). I take "poor in spirit" to mean that we are able to see an achievement-based sense of self-worth for the illusion that is.

Somebody poor in spirit can write because writing is what you seem made to do. Publishing, getting good reviews, making the best-seller lists is beside the point. People poor in spirit don't write, construct buildings, assume public office, or throw a ball to make themselves somebody. They lose themselves in something they seem to have been made to do. They don't need to compete or compare themselves to others. They don't spend enough time in front of the mirror to indulge in self-loathing. They shed a false and probably toxic image of themselves in order to become their true selves. They change their mind about themselves. And some of them do so by changing their mind about who God is.

Changing Our Minds

The heart of the gospel is that God loves us because God loves us. Period. God's infinite, unremitting love brought us out of nothing into being. God's love infuses us at each instant with value that can never be diminished by our circumstances or by what others think of us. When life shatters us, God's love mends us and gives us a new life. Jesus raises us from the dead again and again. So, Jesus shows us that God is a healer, not a blamer. Unfortunately, many of us bear within us the image of a blaming God.

The Bible teaches us that we were created in the image of God. In part, that means that a true understanding of ourselves emerges as we grow in our understanding of God. We don't understand God from an objective distance like an inanimate thing; God is a conscious spiritual being, so we come to know God in personal encounters and intimate relationship. In our relationship with the Holy One, we become who we truly are.

Getting to know God means letting more and more of God into our lives—and letting God in stretches us. As a student in one of my philosophy classes once said, "God is really, really big. We are really, really small." To put it more formally, God is infinite. We are finite. In order to dwell ever more fully in our lives, God stretches our souls again and again. So, our concept of God develops over time. For instance, a preschooler may think of God as a powerful grandparent in the sky. As our mind matures, our experience broadens, and our relationship with God deepens, we refine our image of the divine.

One of the challenges in our human relationships is that we sometimes project ourselves or our parents or some other person from our past onto the person we're trying to understand. We assume that our spouse sees things just as we do, or we hear a judgmental parent when a friend is simply being honest with us. We're not really letting that other person show herself to us. We're projecting an image of who we think she must be onto her.

Just as we project onto other human beings, we sometimes project onto God an image that obscures God's true self from us. That's why thinkers over the centuries have said that we create God in our own image. Some of those thinkers have cast doubt on God's existence. But frequently writers like Reza Aslan are simply making us aware of a human tendency that can frustrate our desire to have an authentic encounter with God.[3] Sometimes deepening our relationship with God means setting aside a distorted or even a toxic idea about who God is.

Many people project their own addiction to blaming onto God. They view God as the Great Blamer. The world is a broken mess, and God intends to fix it. God's strategy for fixing the universe turns on identifying who is to blame for all that's wrong. Punishing the right person will set everything right. As it turns out, everyone is to blame. There is plenty of shame to go around. Everybody deserves punishment. God solves the human problem by punishing Jesus in our place.

But the human problem involves much more than wrongdoing. Our lives are fractured by pain, sorrow, loneliness, and fear. Punishing someone—even punishing Jesus—will not relieve us of grief or mend a shattered relationship. We yearn for God to make us whole, to make our world whole. Sadly, finding someone to blame for our misery seems only to multiply that misery. And crucially, devoting our lives to a blaming God shapes us in that God's image. We continue to look for someone or something to blame to solve the problems that beset us. As long as we blame others, we remain dreadfully susceptible to shame ourselves. Shame is merely blame turned on ourselves. We create ourselves in the image of the Great Blamer and remain caught in a blame-shame loop.

To recover from the blame-shame dynamic, we need to reimagine God. And God initiates our reimagining process in the manger. Christmas wouldn't be Christmas without Nativity scenes. Artisans fashion the holy family from ceramic or wood or stone. Mass-produced plastic figures illuminate front yards. Oxen and donkeys, sheep and cattle fill out the traditional cast of characters. Search the web and you'll see that dinosaurs, zombies, Star Wars figures, and hipsters on Segways have recently paid a visit to the manger. Live Nativity scenes have grown in popularity, especially those designed to provide a drive-through experience.

None of this shows up in the pages of the Bible. Luke tells us only that there were no vacancies in the Bethlehem motels and that Jesus's first crib was a feed trough for barnyard animals. Our imagination has filled in the rest. For some people these depictions of Christ's birth might be cause for a bit of cynicism or scholarly eye-rolling. But I respond differently. After all, God created us with an imagination. And imagination is just what we need to encounter the infinite, omnipotent God in a chubby baby wrapped in tattered rags.

Saint Francis gave us the very first Nativity scene in 1223. Pope Honorious III granted him permission to fill a feed trough with straw and to place it in a cave along with an ox and a donkey. Francis invited the villagers of Grecio, Italy, to look at the scene while he preached about the babe of Bethlehem. In other words, Francis urged the congregation to use not only their senses and their intellect but also their imagination to experience the meaning of the birth of Jesus. I invite you to do something similar. Imagine that an angelic messenger has sent you to encounter God in a new, unlikely way. You've made your way to a barn, and you've found God in the weak and vulnerable flesh of an infant.

Francis believed that the Nativity shows us most clearly who God is and who we are. Franciscan theologians have been influenced by this insight ever since. As a result, they offer us a minority, but still orthodox, view of what God is doing in the manger. Like their fellow theologians from other traditions, Franciscans have asked the question: Why did God become a human being? However, they have arrived at a different answer.

Many Catholic and Protestant thinkers alike have seen Jesus as God's contingency plan. God sent Jesus to die for our sins. Had Adam and Eve never eaten the forbidden fruit, there would have been no Jesus. From this point of view, grace enters the universe as a repair kit. The Franciscans acknowledge that our sins did Jesus in. But Franciscan theologians like John Duns Scotus insist that Jesus was not merely God's response when the creation took a bad turn. On the contrary, when God decided to bring the world into being, Jesus was God's very first thought. That's because the creation is about love from its inception.

God created each rosebush, aardvark, and proton one at a time. Each dog, each star, and each human being is radically unique. No one and nothing is interchangeable. Every creature in this vast universe is completely irreplaceable. God made each being to love that particular being. That includes each and every one of us fragile, coarse, tender, wounded, glorious human beings. To love means to draw near. To get so close that you become one. In Jesus, the divine and the human are so intimately woven together as to be inseparable. That kind of love has been God's aim from all of eternity. And God achieves it in Jesus. So, Jesus changes our mind about God. And by changing our mind about God, Jesus helps us change our minds about ourselves. In Jesus, we see who we truly are as human beings.

We are the beloved, not the blameworthy. As we gradually take hold of ourselves as beloved children of God, shame eventually loses its harsh grip on us. Likewise, we slowly begin to exchange our habit of blaming others for the habit of compassion.

In Christ, we become one with God (theologians call that atonement or at-one-ment). And by being one with God in Christ, we become one with everybody whom God loves. Using blame to off-load our fear or pain or anxiety onto another person is much easier when we see someone else as different. We've grown accustomed to dividing the world into people like me and people not like me: black and white, winner and loser, gay and straight, rural and urban, rich and poor. The challenge for us, once we've learned the lesson of the manger, is to live the truth it has taught us. Everyone we meet is the person God loves, in all his or her breathtaking otherness and bewildering uniqueness. God's love draws us toward unity with each other; no one is blameworthy. As we will see in chapter 5, being accountable is different from being blameworthy. And we are all accountable for our actions. However, shame has no place in any human heart.

From Blame to Compassion

Sadly, blaming does not limit itself to finding a scapegoat for our own inner turmoil. It also cuts us off from compassion for the suffering of others. Instead of feeling empathy, we often blame others for the cruel, heart-rending, or sorrowful circumstances they face. The poor are lazy. Addicts are weak. Lung cancer sufferers smoked for years. Diabetics who have lost their sight or their limbs lack dietary self-control. Under the guise of holding people responsible for their own actions, we turn to faultfinding and emotionally shield ourselves from their misery. After all, it's their own fault. Right?

Jesus teaches us to replace blaming with compassion. Blamers are asking the wrong question. Blamers want to know who is to blame. Find the one at fault and the case is closed. You're off the hook for responding to someone else's something, because you didn't cause it. By contrast, following Jesus involves asking something like this: What role can we play in making this shattered situation whole?

Take for instance the episode in John's Gospel about a man born blind (John 9:1-41). The disciples ask: "Rabbi, who sinned, this man or his parents, that he was born blind?" In other words, who gets the blame for this? Jesus says, "Neither this man nor his parents sinned; he was born blind so that God's works might be revealed in him. We must work the works of him who sent me while it is day."

Some readers jump to the mistaken conclusion that God made the man congenitally blind so that Jesus could pull off a spiffy miracle. Nothing could be further from the truth. The disciples have asked the wrong question about the man's sightlessness. Jesus teaches them to approach the heartaches and injustices and calamities of the world by asking, What will God do about this . . . through us?

Millions of people are sick and hungry, homeless and lonely. Families struggle to nurture and educate handicapped children and to care for elderly parents in declining health. Addiction rates are climbing, and there is a dreadful increase in the number of deaths by drug overdose. These very human needs are our call to action. This is by no means to say that we are to play the part of saviors to helpless victims. On the contrary, Jesus teaches his followers to respect the freedom, dignity, and ability of every human being.

Older models for responding to human need emphasized giving handouts to the "less fortunate." A benefactor condescends to a recipient. This approach promotes dependent behaviors that perpetuate an underclass and hints at a moral gap between the privileged and those in need. By contrast, Jesus reaches out to an equal. Consider how he heals the blind man. Jesus spits on the ground and makes a mud paste to apply to the man's eyes. Jesus literally and figuratively gets his hands dirty with another person's life. He touches a stranger that many—not just the disciples—assume to be at fault for his own disability.

Crucially, Jesus invites the man to cooperate in his own healing. He tells the man, "Go, wash in the pool of Siloam." At no point does Jesus treat the man as a problem to be fixed or an object to be manipulated. Instead, he befriends a stranger, and they work together to bring sight to his eyes. As it turns out, Jesus is far less interested in how we got to where we are than in where we can go from here. When Jesus meets the leprous and the hungry, the lame and the deranged, the hemorrhaging and even the dead, he heals. He loves too urgently to waste time on assigning blame. Jesus is showing us who God really is. And he is showing us who we truly are.

REFLECTION QUESTIONS

1. What idea, image, story, or passage from this chapter grabbed your attention or captured your imagination? How does it connect with or differ from your experience of blame and shame?

2. Recall a time that you felt shame. What story were you telling about yourself at the time? What story were you telling about how God sees you?

3. The author says that God is not the Great Blamer. God loves us and seeks intimacy with us. How do you experience God when things go wrong in your life?

4. Talk about a time that you lost yourself in what you were doing. Where and when does this happen most frequently for you? What do you learn about who you really are when you think about where you lose yourself?

5. The author says that Jesus seeks to change our minds about ourselves by changing our minds about God. Talk about what he might mean by this.

CHAPTER FOUR

MENDING LOSS AND SORROW

Those who do not weep, do not see.

—Victor Hugo, *Les Misérables*

Against our better judgment, Joy, our then high-school-aged son Patrick, and I waded into the post-holiday crowds at a local department store to buy some new place settings. Hordes of other shoppers jammed the aisles. Shuffling and squeezing past them, we finally worked our way to the housewares department. The dishes we chose came in four heavy boxes. As we made our way back to the car through the same mass of shoppers, Patrick carried a box under each arm. I held one box by its handle, switching it from hand to hand as we walked. Joy clutched a box against her chest. Once back in the car, Joy glanced down and gasped. "Oh no! Helen's brooch! It's gone!"

Helen had been Joy's favorite aunt. Unlike Joy's mother, Helen had married later in life. She'd had a career, had traveled to all sorts of interesting places, and regularly joined Joy's family on weekends and vacations. Her wisdom, good humor, and adventurous spirit made Helen a reliable confidante, a mischievous conspirator, and a wise friend. When Helen died, Joy inherited several things. Among them was a circle pin, a sort of brooch inlaid with small diamonds and a pearl. The unassuming, simple elegance of the piece said *Helen*. Joy wore the brooch as an act of love and remembrance.

Losing that brooch was like losing Helen all over again. I could read the grief, regret, and self-blame etched on Joy's face. She said, "I've lost it. It's gone. We'll never find it. Let's just go."

"I'm so sorry," was all I could think to say. I realized that the pin could have fallen anywhere, been picked up by someone else, or accidentally kicked around by dozens of heedless feet to some place we hadn't even gone. Joy's sorrow and resignation were seeping into my own heart.

Patrick spoke up. "We're going back in there. This is important to you. Come on. We're going to find it."

After explaining how impractical and unrealistic searching for the lost brooch would be, Joy finally relented to Patrick's stubborn persistence. To humor him, she let him take her hand and lead her back into the crowds. With Joy in tow, Patrick carefully retraced our steps. Looking off to one side, he spotted the pin. Elated and relieved, Joy laughed and nearly wept. Patrick said matter-of-factly, "I told you we'd find it."

His youthful assurance reminds me of a scene from Kazuo Ishiguro's tender, brutal novel *Never Let Me Go*. The story traces the relationship between three friends from their time as children at Hailsham School into their young adulthood. The narrator, Kathy H., recalls a geography lesson that turns out to provide a keen insight into the human heart.

Reviewing the various areas of Great Britain, the teacher briefly mentioned Norfolk. She explained that it's a peaceful enough place, but jutting out into the sea as it does, people going north and south simply pass it by. So Norfolk is a kind of lost corner of England. Hearing "lost corner," the children began to imagine something that the teacher never intended. Norfolk became for them the place where all lost things wind up. Kathy H. recalled how her friend Ruth explained it: "Ruth said one evening . . . , looking out at the sunset, . . . that 'when we lost something precious, and we'd looked and looked and still couldn't find it, then we didn't have to be completely heartbroken. We still had that last bit of comfort, thinking one day, when we were grown up, and we were free to travel around the country, we could always go and find it again in Norfolk.' "[1]

Patrick was young. His life lay largely ahead of him. He had not yet come to a place of looking back at and taking account of what has been done and what has been left undone. He did not yet bear the ache of things and places and people lost beyond finding. Nor could he have realized that some paths left untaken today could never be walked again.

Our experience that day led me to revisit how I think about loss and sorrow, hope and joy. I had shielded myself from lingering sorrow by moving too quickly to resignation. Patrick's assurance came from an immature confidence that at least temporarily shielded him from sorrow. It gave him the false confidence that everything would turn out just fine. There was no need to mourn the loss of the brooch; we would find it. In our own ways, both Patrick and I wanted to rescue Joy from her sharp sense of loss and to avoid that feeling for ourselves. Neither of us let hope work its mysterious, transforming power. You see, it's in the depths of loss and sorrow that hope brings us to new life.

In the Sermon on the Mount, Jesus famously and paradoxically taught, "Blessed are those who mourn" (Matthew 5:4). Hope does not preempt or prevent mourning. Instead, hope is the voice arising from the depths of sorrow that says, "Your heart is shattered and you are loved beyond reason. Because of this love, the grief you're experiencing, though painful, is also the sign of a heart being mended." And yet, some very sincere Christians fear that deep grief betrays a lack of faith.

Blessed Are Those Who Mourn

Reba and Butch (not their real names) were among the founding members of a congregation that I once served. Butch was in his early eighties. Reba was five or six years younger. When I arrived as their priest, they were still very active. They ably played a variety of leadership roles. Reba and Butch met with me within weeks of my arrival to make sure that I knew that their detailed funeral plans were already on file. They were adamant that their funerals were to be celebrations. A better place awaited them both. All the hymns should be upbeat and the sermon a pep talk. This would be no time for tears.

Their wishes about the funerals were consistent with their charismatic expression of the faith. At least, that was Reba's way. My traditional hymn selection and reverent demeanor as celebrant may have struck her as a little stuffy, but my churchmanship did not deter her from raising and waving her arms in worship. Butch adored Reba. His faith was genuine, but he wasn't the self-reflective type. He was just following her lead in funeral planning, just as he had taken his cue from her in all their years of church life. Both of them assumed that he would die first. That's not how it worked out.

Reba died swiftly of gastrointestinal issues. One day, she was not feeling herself; the next day, an ambulance rushed her to the hospital. Following a major surgery, she had two or three alert days in ICU. And then she breathed her last. Butch was inconsolable. Disoriented. Enraged.

Butch and I were sitting quietly together a day or so before the funeral. He was looking down at the floor. Slowly, he raised his head and said bitterly, "People keep telling me that she's in a better place. To hell with that! She belongs right here with me." All I could say was something like, "You really miss her. It hurts so much." Lame, I know.

Jesus says, "Blessed are those who mourn." Butch could have told you that day that it sure doesn't feel like it. And yet, Jesus assures us that there can be a holiness in our grief. God offers to enter into, and to walk with us through, even our most crushingly painful sorrow. God's compassion turns our grief into the birth process of new life.

Echoing Jesus, the apostle Paul tells the Thessalonians that he does not want them to grieve like those who have no hope (1 Thessalonians 4:13). He didn't say, "I don't want you to grieve." Instead, he helps us to grasp how the resurrection of Christ gives new meaning to our experience of grief. Some Christians have misconstrued Paul's message. They've been taught, or perhaps assumed, that we will be guaranteed entrance into heaven so long as we cling unshakably to the belief that Jesus rose from the dead. Grief, they fear, reveals doubt.

In a misguided attempt to express a sincere faith, quite a few people in the congregations I have served have insisted that, when they die, their funeral should be only a celebration. They want no sadness and certainly no weeping. They envision a sort of liturgical party acknowledging that they've arrived in Paradise. Perhaps they're also trying to be kind by heading off sorrow for the ones they will have left behind. But I have inevitably worried precisely about what such expectations will do to those who have lost a loved one. Do they feel pressure to keep their pain dutifully hidden from view for fear that it doesn't seem Christian or that it would violate their loved one's wishes?

Grief is human. It comes with loving in a world where everything passes away. Sorrow provides an important key to understanding the place of hope in our day-to-day lives. Christianity is about a real God responding to real human life in ways that only God can. We cannot will sorrow away; it is part of the human condition. When we love, the beloved is woven into the fabric of our lives. A loved one's death painfully tears that fabric. God promises to vindicate our love, not by anesthetizing us, but by bringing greater life from the depths of our sorrow. We don't merely get over the death of a loved one as if it were water under the bridge. Even if we anticipate a reunion with someone beyond death's veil—as I do personally—we bear our sense of loss with an ever deeper sense of Christ's life-giving love in our daily lives. I learned this personally with the death of my mother.

The Smell of My Mother's House

A mixture of familiar perfume and stale cigarette smoke hung in the air. Breakfast dishes lay jumbled in the sink atop the previous night's dinner plates and a variety of utensils. The half-full bag in the kitchen garbage had been tied off but not yet taken out. That was my mom. She had taken too long getting ready for work at the deli counter of a nearby grocery, so she had dashed out of her little apartment, promising herself to make the bed, to pick up the towels, to gather the clothes strewn on the floor, and to tidy up the kitchen once she got back home.

It looked to me like she had gone a couple of days like this, expecting to return from work for a cleaning frenzy. She put off tidying up like this from time to time. I couldn't blame her. Her father was a Teutonic neat freak. Leaving a bit of mess always seemed to me to be her way to express her freedom. She preferred order, but she would make it happen in her own good time. Except my mom didn't come back home this time. She died behind the deli counter.

As her only surviving relative, it fell to me to empty her apartment and to deal with her meager estate. After my shifts as a chaplain at Northside Hospital in Atlanta, I would drive to Mom's place. Before moving furniture and cleaning the apartment, I had to sort through her finances.

Her filing system for bank records and bills consisted of piles of opened and unopened envelopes stored in dresser drawers, piled on the coffee table, and stacked on the kitchen counter. Hours ticked by as I sorted through page after page of outdated documents. Alongside these impersonal papers, I found pictures, cards, and old newspaper clippings that she had saved. They were mostly about me or about the both of us. Each of her mementos stopped me in my tracks and slowed my progress.

The thick smell of the place affected my breathing. It saturated my clothes and my hair. On an especially hot July Atlanta evening, I dragged back into the house we were sitting for the summer. Joy was pregnant with our third child, Patrick. She was in the kitchen with our seven-year-old son, Andrew, and our toddler, Meredith.

"How you doing, kid?" Joy asked.

"I stink," I said. "I just reek of my mother's house."

What I realize now is that "I stink" was easier to say than "I miss my mother."

I didn't idolize my mother. I had no illusion that she was a Norman Rockwell figure of orderliness, good grace, and unflappable wisdom. Her love for me was extravagant and sloppy. Our relationship was messy. Like her apartment. We supported each other and pulled for each other and stuck by each other and occasionally poked each other in the eye. Maybe you've come across or even achieved something different. But that's what love has looked like in my life: imperfect people embracing and frustrating, nurturing and infuriating imperfect people.

And it seems to me that Jesus makes this way of messy love into the way of eternal life. That's what I hear when he says, "I am the way, and the truth, and the life" (John 14:6). Consider the context. Jesus says these words on the night before he is crucified. The disciples have just shared the Last Supper. In other words, Jesus has instituted the Holy Eucharist as the definitive spiritual practice for his community. The Eucharist is not just some prayer we say or some rite we perform; it is the Holy Meal in which we participate in the divine life and the divine life abides in us. The Holy Meal at once shows us who we are and makes us who we are.

In Matthew, Mark, and Luke, Jesus uses the familiar words "This is my body" and "This is my blood" to establish the meaning of the Eucharist. John, by contrast, records that Jesus washed the feet of his disciples and instructed them to do the same for each other. The foot washing tells us the meaning of the Eucharist (John 13:1-9).

After supper, Jesus tells the disciples that he is going away. He will die, rise, and ascend. And he adds that they know the way his is going. Thomas says he doesn't know any such thing. And Jesus says, "Yes you do! I just showed you. That was the point of that whole foot-washing thing!" The foot washing signifies the Way of Jesus. We all come together with dirt between our toes. No exceptions. We imperfect people accept and nurture and bear with other imperfect people. People with dirty feet wash people with dirty feet. And yes, we will get each other's dirt on each other in the process of getting clean. Our hands will retain the smell of each other's feet. Christ himself resides in the very flesh of those who wash and those who need to be washed. This is the Way. It is the only way to the heart of God. Eternal life starts here.

Back in the kitchen with Joy and Andrew and Meredith, the words "I stink" seemed to hang in the air for a few minutes. Nobody spoke. And then my seven-year-old son, Andrew, spoke up. "You don't stink, Dad. You smell like Oma."

Unconventional Grief

When we think about grief, the death of a loved one usually comes to mind. Some of us also rightly associate grief with other kinds of loss. Relationships dissolve, health fails, careers flounder. With each loss, we mourn a life that was. A life that we shared. A life that was ours. In each of these experiences of grief, something or someone is gone. Absence gnaws a ragged hole in our souls. But there is another kind of grief. I have heard it called "unconventional grief."[2] And I have seen it firsthand many times.

For instance, on one of my regular visits to a skilled care facility, I walked by a man and a woman huddled close together at the edge of a common area. The woman sat serenely in a wheelchair, smiling vacantly at the man. The man—her husband, I assumed—had placed a small tape player on an adjacent table. Big band tunes drifted from the tiny speaker. I heard him say to her tenderly, "You remember this one. Don't you?" Then he sang wistfully along for a couple of bars. "You remember. This was our song."

Unconventional grief occurs when the person we've lost is still right in front of us. A loved one may drift into dementia or sink into addiction. A person we once knew can be spirited away from us by brain injury or mental illness. The one we love is gone. And still sits at the Thanksgiving table. This kind of sorrow is not the same as anticipating someone's death. Walking with loved ones through their final months or weeks or days is a tender experience all its own. A loss is coming, and it will be sharply painful. By contrast, unconventional grief involves continuing to live with a person who has become a stranger or to whom you are now a stranger.

What do we do with this kind of sorrow? More specifically, does our belief in the resurrection of Christ offer a perspective that helps make sense of life in the midst of ongoing sorrow?

Sometimes, Christians make do with a flawed coping strategy. They believe that a carefree paradise awaits believers after death. All suffering is temporary. In heaven, we won't suffer any more. We'll be happy as little celestial clams. None of our earthly sorrows will matter anymore. And there lies the problem with this coping strategy. What do you mean that our earthly sorrows won't matter anymore? So, none of the heartache that comes with loving these people actually makes a difference? We just have to wait it out, and then we can forget all about it?

I believe in eternal life. Jesus-followers are resurrection people. But I don't for one minute believe that the resurrection diminishes the importance of our mortal suffering. On the contrary, the resurrection saturates even the most sorrowful moments of our lives with significance.

Following Jesus is all about learning to care with abandon. That's the very essence of eternal life: unguarded, relentless compassion. That kind of caring is going to leave a mark. In your hands. And feet. And side. The resurrection vindicates a life utterly given over to care. The resurrection assures us that even our deepest wounds—our most grievous sorrows—have deep significance. Sorrow in the name of love is the Way of the Cross. That Way leads to the empty tomb.

Riffing on an image from the apostle Paul, you could say that, in Christ, the tomb becomes the womb of eternal life. He suggested something like this in his letter to the Thessalonians (1 Thessalonians 5:3). It can be easy to forget that Paul's letters were mostly pastoral responses to the life struggles of real people.

The tiny congregation of Thessalonica had been in existence for only a brief time. Its members included both Jews and Gentiles. Paul had been forced to move on from Thessalonica while the congregation was still in its theological infancy. His teachings were radically new. The members had brought with them to this new faith a stew of ideas and practices about life after death from their various backgrounds. Getting their collective head around the resurrection was taking time.

Apparently they were waiting expectantly for the imminent return of Jesus. They had concluded that living believers would greet Jesus and receive eternal life. Unfortunately, Jesus was taking his sweet time about the return trip. In the meantime, people were dying, people they loved. What would happen to those who had already died? Or, to put it another way, they wanted to know how the faith would give meaning to their sorrow.

Paul responds that the resurrection is for both the living and the dead. The Day of the Lord will come like labor pains on a pregnant woman. Now, in his words to the Thessalonians, Paul seems to suggest that God will come back suddenly and settle scores. But in his letter to the Romans, Paul talks about those labor pains in a different way. He says, "We know that the whole creation has been groaning in labor pains until now" (Romans 8:22).

In other words, God responds to our suffering. Joins us in our suffering. Transforms our suffering. Vindicates our suffering. In Jesus, compassion's heartbreak gives birth to an entirely new kind of life. A life that passes through death and beyond the grave again. To love—even when that love is breaking our heart—means something. Holiness happens there. We humans naturally wonder what to do with our sorrow. Jesus teaches us to wonder expectantly what God is doing with it. And then he tells us that, whatever it is that God will do, God will do it through our compassion for one another.

Show Up and Look Alert

Eighty percent of life is showing up. Some give Woody Allen credit for the quip. A Google search will give you a few variants. The word order changes. You'll find "success" substituted for "life." One of my pastoral care mentors taught me her own variant. "Show up and look alert." Her old adage still resonates with me. And now as a bishop I regularly commend it to my clergy colleagues.

Initially, the phrase guided me as I walked with my parishioners through loss. The death of a parent, a spouse, or a child. Suicides and drug overdoses. Diminished mobility from car crashes and falls and strokes. A cancer diagnosis. Divorce. Long-term unemployment. Stalled careers. Dreams unfulfilled.

Loss comes in many forms. Whatever shape it takes, loss leaves grief or regret or remorse or shock or some mixture of these in its wake. No one's pastoral bag of tricks comes with a magic wand. We cannot make another person's sorrow vanish. Instead of fixing things, though, we are able to show up and look alert. Getting ourselves to the right address at the right time is no small thing. But showing up and looking alert serves as shorthand for something far deeper. It refers to compassion. And compassion is rooted in empathy.

Empathy differs from sympathy. We can recognize another person's pain without involving our whole selves with that person. It's sort of like saying, "Wow! That's bad for you. Sure hope it gets better. Let me know what I can do. Thoughts and prayers." Sympathy does not require that we realize that we've been there too. And we don't have to be vulnerable to another person's life just to acknowledge that the person is suffering and offer him or her a hand.

Connection is at the core of empathy. In empathy, we do more than recognize the ache in another person's heart; we connect with that person because we've been to that dreadful place too. We say, "I'm in this thing with you. My heart is breaking along with you, and God willing, my heart will eventually rejoice with yours." Compassion doesn't involve making the other person's pain our own, but by being compassionate, we have made ourselves vulnerable to someone else. And we have committed to walk with that person through the valley of the shadow of whatever as long as that's the path the person's on.

Strictly speaking, I think that's what love is. Showing up and looking alert. Life, as it turns out, is love. If you don't love, you're slowly dying inside. So, what I took initially to be an adage for pastoral care is actually a lesson for all of us. It's the lesson with which Jesus began his ministry: "Repent, for the kingdom of heaven has come near" (Matthew 4:17).

Some readers of that passage won't glean anything like an adage about presence in it. Instead, they hear a dire warning. Maybe even a threat.

They interpret Jesus's words to mean something like this: "Time is short. Judgment is near. Unless you want to burn in hell, clean up your act and acknowledge Jesus as the Only Way." By contrast, I hear something more like this. "The loving presence of God is already near you. All around you. Be open to it. Let go of whatever obscures the divine presence from you or lets you distance yourself from it." To put that another way, God's love is coursing through the people and the animals and the plants and the sunsets and the starry skies and the fuzzy slippers of your everyday life. Show up, and look alert.

Jesus makes abundantly clear that this is especially the case in the suffering of others. Paradoxically, when we reach out in compassion, we are not finding God; God is finding us. And the experience of being found by the holy heals our deepest sense of loss. Eventually. God has already shown up. It's on us to show up too. Showing up and looking alert is our spiritual work. Jesus taught us this lesson with what some call the parable of the wise and the foolish bridesmaids (Matthew 25:1-13).

The story goes like this. Ten bridesmaids went out to meet the bridegroom. They didn't know his precise arrival time. Half the women prepared themselves for a lengthy delay. They loaded up on extra oil for their lamps. The other five women brought lamps but no extra oil. Sure enough, the bridegroom took his own sweet time getting there. The sun set. Lamps were lit. Sleep overcame the women. At midnight, somebody roused the group with the news that the bridegroom was just around the bend. By this time, all the lamps were sputtering out.

Five of the bridesmaids reloaded their lamps. Those who had brought no extra oil asked their sisters to share their oil. The well-stocked bridesmaids explained that they hadn't brought enough to share. So the oil-less women ran frantically to Walmart to get more fuel for their lamps. The bridegroom arrived while the shoppers were still away. They missed the bridegroom. Missed the wedding. And got barred from the reception.

Let's remember that parables are not allegories. When Jesus tells a parable, he's not asking us to draw an analogy between elements in the story and things in the world. For instance, you don't have to assume— you probably shouldn't assume—that the bridegroom stands for Jesus. I realize that we've all heard interpretations of this parable that hinge on the bridegroom being Jesus. Frequently, such a reading accompanies the assumption that the kingdom of heaven is where believers go after they die. Hell, of course, is the alternative celestial address left for unbelievers. The point of the parable becomes this: accept Jesus as Lord before it's too late. Even if you do mishandle the parable as if it were an allegory, this reading would remain unconvincing to me. But once you commit to hearing the parable as a parable, you'll come away with some very different messages. Parables are unsettling stories that invite us to rethink some of our basic assumptions.

From the start, Jesus tells us that this parable is about the Kingdom. The Kingdom is wherever God's love is shaking things up and bringing things to new life. So with this parable Jesus is drawing us into revisiting where we think we will encounter God. One implication of the story is that the Kingdom is nearer than you think. It's already on top of you. If you delay, you'll miss it. It's right in front of your nose. The child's need to be loved when showing off a picture she drew at school. A friend's anxiety masked by his off-putting anger. No one else can notice this, encounter this, engage this Kingdom for you. I can't lend you my extra oil. I can't just tell you about it. You have to be there. The genuine encounter is always personal.

The Kingdom comes in unrepeatable moments. We can be so preoccupied or indifferent or fearful that we simply miss those moments. This is especially true when we encounter another's wounded soul. Jesus isn't condemning us for inattentiveness. Instead, he's helping us see that we're missing resurrection moments. Moments in which our compassion draws us into new life.

I've spent much of my ordained life being present to others in their suffering and sorrow. Eventually I realized that when I make myself vulnerable to the pain of another person, I'm also making myself available to the resurrection. To new, God-given life. In my compassion for others, I see with great clarity that, with every loss, a larger or smaller bit of me has died. When the Kingdom draws near—when God shows up and looks alert—God leaves new life in the divine wake.

REFLECTION QUESTIONS

1. What idea, image, story, or passage from this chapter grabbed your attention or captured your imagination? How does it connect with or differ from your experience with loss and sorrow?

2. Discuss how the author interprets Jesus's teaching: blessed are those who mourn.

3. The author says that, through God, we experience the resurrection in the depths of our sorrow. Recall an experience of grief. How did God respond to you in the midst of your grief?

4. We also experience the power of the resurrection in our compassion for those in mourning. Talk about a time that you sat with someone else in his or her grief. What did you learn about God's love and how did it affect your life?

5. Has someone else's compassion for you been a source of healing for you? Share that experience.

CHAPTER FIVE

FORGIVENESS, PASSION, AND JUSTICE

As you press on for justice, be sure to move with dignity and discipline, using only the weapon of love.

—Martin Luther King Jr., "Paul's Letter to American Christians"

When Thordis Elva was sixteen, she got to know Tom Stranger. They were performing together in a school play. Tom was an eighteen-year-old Australian exchange student still struggling to get the hang of Iceland's language and customs. The two grew close. At school, they would meet for lunch to talk and to hold hands. Thordis was in love for the first time. After about a month, they attended the school's Christmas Ball together. She was thrilled.[1]

At the ball she drank rum for the first time, got drunk, and grew terribly ill. The security guards offered to get her an ambulance. She refused after Tom volunteered to take her back home. Tom carried her to her room. He placed her on her bed, took off her clothes, and raped her.

The next day, she was in severe physical pain. Her soul was in torment. She felt shame and betrayal. She blamed herself. Weeks passed before she could name for herself that Tom had raped her. By that time, he had returned to his native Australia.

For years, she lurched through life in silent agony. She carried a pen and a notebook wherever she went, just to have something to do with her hands. One day, sitting in a café, she put pen to paper in her usual nervous way. To her astonishment, a letter to Tom flowed onto the page. She detailed what he had done to her and how it had devastated her life. But what shocked Thordis most was this thought: she yearned to find a way to forgive Tom. She realized that Tom might not be willing to admit his guilt or to make amends. Nevertheless, she recognized that forgiveness was her path to liberation and peace. And so her long, uneven journey of forgiveness began in earnest.

Forgiveness and Reconciliation

Forgiveness does not excuse wrongdoing. On the contrary, holding those who have injured us accountable for their actions is crucial to forgiveness. And yet, to forgive is to refuse to yield to vengeful impulses to inflict pain on those who have caused us harm. We seek justice without indulging in revenge. I will discuss justice in more detail later in this chapter. But for now, suffice it to say that refusing to take revenge is not equivalent to saying, "That's OK." On the contrary, saying, "I forgive you," also implies, "That's not OK. Do not do that again."

And yet, wresting an apology from the person who has hurt us is not the aim of forgiveness as such. Sincere apologies are a good thing. They are necessary for moving forgiveness toward reconciliation. I'll get to that in a moment. But first let's be honest about something. Not all people will admit that they have done us harm. When others are unrepentant for the pain they have caused, forgiving them can be very difficult. But it's important to remember that forgiveness is not a response to someone else's contrition. Otherwise, we could be held emotionally hostage forever to people who couldn't care less that they have done us harm. We forgive because we see the goodness and the freedom of being a forgiving person.

Jesus talked at length about forgiveness. Once, Peter asked him, "So, look, how often do I have to forgive? Seven times? Will that about cut it?" Imagine the look on Peter's face when Jesus said, "Make that seventy-seven times" (Matthew 18:21-22). Strictly speaking, Jesus was not setting an upper limit on the number of times Peter would have to forgive a repeat offender. He was telling him—telling us—how forgiveness works. Forgiveness is a habit of the soul that we develop. It is a spiritual practice that we refine over time.

Think of forgiveness as a virtue. Aristotle defined virtue as a habit of thinking, feeling, and acting. It's a motion of the whole person. The word *virtue* and the word *virtuoso* come from the same linguistic root. So, a virtuous person is a virtuoso at being a human being. Jesus is teaching us that becoming fully human involves becoming a forgiving person. In response to an insult or an injury, a wise, spiritually mature person will think, feel, and act in a forgiving way as second nature.

This does not mean that forgiveness simply becomes automatic. But for someone practiced in forgiving, forsaking retaliation is far more than a discrete act of will. The force of habit moves us in a direction. Take an analogy from baseball. Some of us have imagined being the batter who drives in the winning run in the bottom of the ninth inning. Fewer of us have imagined being the player who spends hour upon hour in the batting cage practicing our swing in order to make that one moment in a game possible. But professional baseball players will tell you that driving in the winning run in that game was the culmination of all those hours of practice.

Everyday life is our spiritual batting cage. Our many acts of forgiveness for minor day-to-day hurts and slights can prepare us to meet grievous wounds with forgiveness instead of revenge.

Forgiving deep wounds is not like flipping a spiritual switch. Forgiveness is a process. Even when we work to leave grievances and resentments behind, they can resurface from time to time. Maybe they're triggered by someone's offhand remark or by an old tune from back in the day. Sometimes the pain of an old wound seems to come out of nowhere. The persistence of our grievances makes sense when we remember that we're not objective judges deciding whether or not to grant a suspended sentence to an offender; instead, we are shattered people. Forgiveness is the way in which we participate in the divine love that mends us. And even divine mending takes time. As people in twelve-step programs might put it, we forgive one day at a time.

On the day in the café that Thordis decided to find forgiveness for Tom, she started what would be an eight-year process. Courageously, she began an email correspondence with her attacker. They exchanged deeply honest, painful truth with each other. And while Thordis could see that she had made significant progress, she also yearned for a closure she had not yet experienced. So she invited Tom to meet face-to-face for a weeklong conversation.

Tom agreed. They each traveled to Cape Town, South Africa. They chose the site in part because it was a midway point. But more important, no place on this planet has participated more intentionally in a process of public reconciliation than the former home of Apartheid. In the TED talk she shared with Tom, Thordis said that, as the jet's wheels touched down, she thought, *Why didn't I just get a therapist and a bottle of vodka like a normal person?* Forgiveness is frequently a long and winding road.

As Thordis's journey illustrates, forgiveness involves leaning into our pain, staying with our hurt and devastation long enough to name what we are feeling, and identifying how our woundedness is diminishing our lives. Admitting that we are wounded makes us vulnerable and requires deep spiritual courage. The trajectory of forgiveness also leads to reconciliation. When Thordis speaks of seeking closure, I believe this is what she yearned for. Reconciliation is the restoration of a shattered relationship.

Reconciliation does not bring us back to the way things used to be. Thordis had no desire to be Tom's girlfriend or to forget that any of this had happened. She understood that some sort of new relationship—built honestly and painstakingly upon the ruins of the past—would bring the closure she longed for. But reconciliation was not something that Thordis could achieve alone. Tom would have to be part of the process.

Forgiveness can be a one-way street. I can forgive you even if you show no regret about the injury you've done me. When we forgive an unrepentant person, forgiveness takes the form of reinforced boundaries and keeping a safe distance. Our relationship will remain strained at best, and may even be shattered. For instance, my father never admitted to abusing my mother, and he showed no signs of being contrite. Nevertheless, my mother forgave him. She moved to another town, started a new life, and interacted with him only when some issue about my care required it. She sought no revenge, but she knew to remain guarded.

By contrast, reconciliation is always reciprocal. The injured person's forgiveness is met with genuine remorse and amended behavior. While the relationship will probably not return to what it was like before it was broken, a new kind of relationship can gradually emerge. It may seem paradoxical, but forgiveness can transform both the person who forgives and the person who is forgiven.

Through her conversations with Tom, Thordis underwent a metamorphosis. No longer a victim, she is now a courageous survivor. Emerging from her own pain and emotional devastation, Thordis came to a new sense of solidarity with the millions of women who have suffered sexual violence. She exemplifies the wounded healer that Henri Nouwen describes in the widely loved book by the same title.[2] Echoing that book's theme, a daily reflection at the Nouwen website put it this way:

> Nobody escapes being wounded. We all are wounded people, whether physically, emotionally, mentally, or spiritually. The main question is not "How can we hide our wounds?" so we don't have to be embarrassed, but "How can we put our woundedness in the service of others?" When our wounds cease to be a source of shame, and become a source of healing, we have become wounded healers.[3]

In her writing and speaking career, Thordis draws upon her own experiences to help other women find a new life. She shows us that forgiveness can transform our own suffering into compassion for other wounded individuals.

While Thordis may not characterize her lectures and workshops in these terms, her activities arguably fit the description of what many Christians have called works of mercy. Motivated by compassion, she seeks to alleviate the suffering of rape survivors. The traditional list of works of mercy includes feeding the hungry, sheltering the homeless, and visiting prisoners. Workers at soup kitchens and battered women's shelters, community medical clinics and rehab centers seek to comfort and to heal those who have been wounded, forgotten, and marginalized. Thordis's mission to restore survivors of rape to wholeness can be justifiably added to this list of ministries.

Compassion connects us to the woundedness of another soul and moves us to offer healing and comfort. And that is where works of mercy stop: the relief of another individual's misery. Even when Thordis addresses an auditorium full of survivors or anyone serves hundreds of people at a soup kitchen, they are still focused on relieving the suffering of a large number of individuals on that particular day. When they have helped those individuals, they have done all that there is to do.

Helping others in need is holy and noble work. However, for many of us, long experience with works of mercy begins to feel like we are treating a symptom without addressing an underlying cause. Week after week, we feed hungry people and see no decrease in their numbers. On the contrary, some of us are noticing an increase in those lacking proper nutrition. In the case of those who join Thordis in working with women who have survived rape, I suspect that there has been no decline in demand for their services. On the contrary, the enormity and regularity of sexual abuse and exploitation is still being uncovered.

When we begin to experience this kind of spiritual dissonance, we are no longer satisfied to ask, How can I help this person? Instead, some of us ask, Why are there so many people wounded in this way? With this question, we can undergo a shift in consciousness. Our compassion expands into a passion for justice.

A Passion for Justice

Author Ronald Rolheiser illustrates the move from pastoral compassion to a passion for social justice in the form of a story that some call the parable of the river:

Once upon a time there was a town which was built beyond the bend in a river. One day some of its children were playing by the river when they spotted three bodies floating in the water. They ran to get help and the townsfolk quickly pulled the bodies from the river. One body was dead so they buried it. One was alive, but quite ill, so they put it into the hospital. The third was a healthy child, so they placed it in a family who cared for it and took it to school. From that day on, each day a number of bodies came floating around the bend in the river and, each day, the good charitable townspeople pulled them out and tended to them—burying the dead, caring for the sick, finding homes for the children, and so on. This went on for years, and the townspeople came to expect that each day would bring its quota of bodies . . . but, during those years, nobody thought to walk up the river, beyond the bend, and check out why, daily, those bodies came floating down the river.[4]

A passion for a just society begins when it occurs to us to go up the river. We see the suffering and the deprivation around us and look for the underlying causes in our social, economic, legal, and political structures.

In October of 2017, the hashtag #metoo went viral. Thousands upon thousands of women—actresses, politicians, waitresses, executives, and hotel workers—came forward with stories of sexual abuse and exploitation. They brought to our attention not merely a series of isolated instances of sexual violence and oppression, but a social, economic, and political system whose abiding structures debase and devalue women. The women who shared their stories offered more than comfort and solace for fellow victims. They sought—and continue to seek—to change the world that creates so many victims.

The #metoo movement urges us to go up river. The civil rights movement of the 1950s and 1960s, the antiwar movement during the Vietnam War, and the Black Lives Matter movement today are animated by the

71

same passion for justice. These movements show us the trajectory that our forgiveness work can take. Suffering becomes compassion. Compassion can lead us to an abiding passion for justice. Our individual acts of forgiveness bring us into solidarity with others in pain, and our sense of solidarity can open us to God's dream for everyone. In Christ, God is renewing the entire creation. God's dream is a new heaven and a new earth shining with perfect justice and unbroken peace: a creation in which human dignity is never diminished and God's love cannot be doubted because its presence is undeniable in how we love one another. In other words, when Jesus teaches us to forgive, he is drawing us into a holy passion for reconciliation on planet Earth.

Passion energizes us. It moves us. Poets and songwriters frequently use fire as a metaphor for passion. And yet, fire also has a dangerous and destructive side. Fire warms us in the cold and pushes back the darkness at night. But, those same flames can reduce our homes to ashes and consume our flesh. Like fire, passion can create and it can destroy. Forgiveness does not extinguish passion. On the contrary, forgiveness is the spiritual work by which our passion becomes the creative force that motivates us to restore fractured relationships. Once we've "gone up the river," to use Rolheiser's image, passion urges us toward establishing justice for all. That includes the ones who have accumulated and protected their own social status, political power, and economic privilege at the expense of others. However, passion can also take the form of habitual rage, violence, and destructive vengeance.

Theologians and philosophers have recognized passion's power and danger for centuries. Some, like the Stoics, saw nothing but trouble in the passions, especially anger. They advocated a dispassionate response to life's changing circumstances. Mr. Spock of the Star Trek films exemplifies the Stoic ideal. He seeks to become entirely rational and to remain untouched by his emotions. His famous response to even the most dire situation is, "Fascinating!"

When we are injured, abused, or exploited, our passion frequently comes in the form of anger. And Christian tradition has struggled to see how anger could be a healthy human expression. The early Church passed down to later generations a list of seven deadly sins. Wrath takes its place among envy and pride and the like. Frequently we see "anger" substituted for "wrath." As a younger man, I misinterpreted the list's message to mean that all expressions of anger were sinful. I was struggling to come to terms with the anger that I was carrying forward from childhood experiences. The Church seemed to be saying to me, "Just don't feel that way." Stuffing my anger, I alternated between self-loathing and occasional outbursts. In my years of pastoral work, I discovered that I am not alone in this and that there is a better way.

There is no question that habitual anger, resentment, and explosive rage can burn innocent bystanders and scorch the earth. In the Sermon on the Mount, Jesus himself warns us about anger that dehumanizes other people. He says that contempt for another person—saying "You fool!"—tramples on the respect due every human being. Dehumanizing someone, especially a class of someones, sets us on the path to oppression and violence. Those who indulge in scorn for their neighbor are "liable to the hell of fire." While some will hear Jesus saying that God will punish us for being angry, I take his words to mean something different. Anger is a fire that can consume not only the neighbor we hate but the heart that lights the flame in the first place. Our own anger can consume us in the end. No wonder Jesus urges us to turn the other cheek and to love our enemy (Matthew 5:21-22; 5:39; 5:43-44).

And yet, in another context, Jesus says that he has come "to bring fire to the earth" (Luke 12:49) In her book *Wearing God*, Lauren Winner hears this passage as Jesus's desire to ignite the world with love—with passion—for God and everything that God loves. She reads the passage this way: "I have come to set alight your ardor for Me and for all things good and lovely, and I wish that fire were already lit."[5] To put it in terms that may remind some of Hildegard of Bingen, Jesus is the fire at the heart of everything, kindling the creation from within. That fire brings humans and pelicans, longleaf pines and fire ants into being and stretches them toward mature grace and beauty. And it is the holy fire that will bring justice to the world. Jesus means for us to be infused with that fire.

Some kinds of anger diminish us every time. Reactivity—a sort of knee-jerk striking out when we're injured or afraid—is lizard-brain stuff. Its operating principle is, *You hurt me and I'll hurt you worse.* Similarly, habitual resentment eats away at us from the inside. Just ask recovering alcoholics or addicts where nursing their resentments has gotten them. *Relapse* is probably the first word many of them will say.

By contrast, the prophets embodied a kind of holy anger when criticizing Israel for its neglect, oppression, and abuse of the poor. Jesus himself embodied righteous indignation. He told hypocritical, politically motivated religious leaders that they were like whitewashed tombs (Matthew 23:27). He drove the money changers from the Temple with a whip, overturning tables and causing quite a scene (John 2:13-15). When we follow Jesus, we will at times express this kind of holy anger as well. Righteous indignation targets injustice and fuels our ability to persist in the long, uneven process of making this world a better place.

But here is the challenge that Jesus's example sets at least for me. He was able to denounce injustice and hold the unjust accountable without losing sight of the dignity of every human being, even those human beings forgetful of the dignity of others. Paradoxically, Jesus's mission was to restore the dignity of each human individual and all of human common life. Nothing degrades our human dignity like our refusal to recognize it in each other. This is especially true when we're fighting for the human dignity of the oppressed and marginalized.

At times, it's a stretch for me to recognize the dignity of predatory religious figures, self-serving elected officials, and hateful white supremacists. In other words, self-righteousness sometimes threatens to overtake my righteous indignation. Maybe you've found a similar dynamic in your own soul. This is not to say that we should surrender in our insistence upon justice for all. There is much work to do to repair the torn fabric of the world. However, even as we work steadily to dismantle unjust social, political, and economic systems, we must be careful to do so in a way that does not make us as individuals into who we do not want to be. We should seek to employ a strategy consistent with our desire to inhabit souls defined by the habits of loving and forgiving.

REFLECTION QUESTIONS

1. What idea, image, story, or passage from this chapter grabbed your attention or captured your imagination? How does it affirm, challenge, conflict with, or expand how you've been thinking about forgiveness?
2. Talk about a time that you struggled to forgive someone else. What acted as obstacles to your ability to forgive and what helped you to move toward forgiveness?
3. The author distinguishes between forgiveness and reconciliation. Talk about that distinction. Have you forgiven people with whom you could not find reconciliation? Have you been able to be reconciled with another person who wounded you?
4. Have you ever struggled with anger when someone has wounded you? Were you able to move past that anger to forgiveness? Share your experience.
5. The author says that learning the habit of forgiveness can lead to a desire for justice. Discuss what the author means by justice.

CHAPTER SIX

Just Us

If we are to love our neighbors, before doing anything else we must see our neighbors. With our imagination as well as our eyes, that is to say like artists, we must see not just their faces but the life behind and within their faces. Here it is love that is the frame we see them in.

—Frederick Buechner, *Whistling in the Dark*

C ollette Divito couldn't get a job as a professional baker. Many of the applications she submitted got a similar response. "Your skills are great. You're just not a good fit for our company." Undaunted, Collette started her own business baking and selling cookies. With the help of social media and local news coverage, Collette's home-based bakery picked up local clients and began getting mail orders from around the country. If the proof is in the pudding—or, in Collette's case, in the baked goods—Collette has plenty of ability. People can't get enough of her cinnamon-dipped chocolate chip cookies. So you have to wonder what this "fit for our company" issue was.[1]

I don't know Collette personally. And I've read no reports about why the Boston-area bakeries to which she applied—and apparently she applied to all of them—thought she wouldn't fit into their operation. But I can say a few things about Collette on the basis of a news clip that I watched. She's in her upper twenties and brunette. Her eyes twinkle when she smiles and, at least in front of the camera, she smiles a lot. If moonwalking in the kitchen is any indication, she's unselfconsciously playful. And she has Down syndrome.

My guess is that it was not the color of her hair or the so-so quality of her moonwalk that turned off prospective employers. They may not have seen Collette at all. Instead, store managers may have seen their own outdated assumptions and expectations about people with Down syndrome. Take the old phrase "What you see is what you get."[2] In *Pilgrim at Tinker Creek*, Annie Dillard didn't use it to mean, "What is, is." Instead, she was saying that all of us need to learn to see, to really see, what is right in front of us. Otherwise we will miss the subtle textures and delicate hues of which our world is composed. We will merely skim the surface of a reality that contains inexhaustible, intoxicating depths. We will see only what our eyes can glimpse through the portals of our narrow minds. Through steady practice, Dillard came to see with intricate detail the life of the individual insects and animals and plants surrounding her cabin in Tinker Creek, Virginia.

Jesus urges us to use the same tender care and gracious attentiveness that Dillard used to see her natural surroundings—to see, *really* see, the human beings right in front of us. The apostle Paul teaches us that the resurrection refines and deepens our perception of other people. He realized that the citizens of his Hellenistic world were not really seeing people for who they were. Instead, they tended to divide people into Jew or Greek, slave or free, friend or foe (Galatians 3:28). Into *us* versus *them*. By contrast, he says, "From now on, therefore, we regard no one from a human point of view; even though we once knew Christ from a human point of view, we know him no longer in that way. So if anyone is in Christ, there is a new creation" (2 Corinthians 5:16-17a). From the perspective of the resurrection, there is just us. There is no longer an *us* opposed to a *them*. We are one.

Alas, our vision is still frequently distorted. As authors Diana Butler Bass and Brian McLaren have both noted, we still yield to what is an ancient tribal impulse: an impulse that God has been transforming since at least the time of Abraham.[3]

A New Kind of Tribe

God called Abraham and Sarah to leave their family and to start a new one. Actually, they were leaving their tribe. In Abraham's day, everybody was part of a tribe composed basically of his extended family. Almost nobody left his tribe. So this already makes Abraham's story pretty unusual.

All other tribes were competitors, if not enemies; even allies were potential adversaries. Violent clashes between tribes for land and resources were the norm. Each tribe would do whatever it took to protect its way of life and to enhance its position among the tribes. Their conflicts could reach a nauseating level of savagery. A conquering force would sometimes slaughter every man, woman, and child of the enemy. Or, the victors might put all the males to death and take the women for themselves. In any event, they didn't want any males or male heirs left to plot future retaliation. And get this: the winners all said that God told them to do it.

God sent Abraham and Sarah to a distant land to start a new tribe. Tribes came to be by having children, and that's why God promised Abraham and Sarah that they would have a veritable Milky Way of kids. God didn't intend for Abraham to start a tribe that was just like other tribes, only stronger. God wasn't going to equip Abraham with a bigger military force and more advanced weapons. All the other tribes were dedicated to taking what they could get and defending what they had accumulated. Every existing tribe was entirely self-interested. Abraham's new tribe was to grow from a radically new idea. Here's how God explained it to Abraham. "You will be a blessing. . . . In you all the families of the earth shall be blessed" (Genesis 12:2b, 3b). Abraham was not starting up just one more tribe. He was going to be the father of an entirely new kind of tribe. That tribe's purpose was to bless all comers. To restore God's peace to creation. To end us-versus-them consciousness once and for all.

The apostle Paul believed that Abraham's story continued in Christ. In Christ, all the tribes of the world will be blessed. As Christ's body, his followers are a new kind of tribe that exists to bring God's healing to the creation. Paul took up the holy call to overcome us-versus-them thinking. He urges us to enter into the incomparable mystery that is each individual human being. Paul coaxes us to recognize the Spirit that inhabits each of us in an infinite variety of ways. Paul put it this way: we are all members of one Body. Each member is different from all the others. And yet all of these unique members are woven into one Body because we are inhabited by and animated by one Spirit (1 Corinthians 12:4-26).

We need each other in order to be who we most truly are. No two members of the Body are interchangeable. The foot cannot serve as a hand. Even the right hand cannot replace the left hand. No member of the Body is disposable. Each member of the Body works together with the other members of the Body for the sake of a common purpose. Members of the Body cannot be what they are without cooperating with the other members. For instance, the eye cannot catch without the hand. And the hand needs the eye's guidance to catch.

To put this another way, being human is a group project. To know ourselves and to be ourselves involves fitting with all other human beings in a common undertaking. Inhabited, empowered, and guided by the same Spirit, we are the hands and the feet that are healing and nurturing and renewing the world. The hearts and eyes of mercy and compassion, justice and peace. Everyone is indispensable and irreplaceable. Everyone fits. At least, that is where the trajectory of a resurrection-shaped life leads.

Paul was not naive about Roman rule; he realized that the world had not yet arrived at this destination in his day. Mercilessly leveraging their military superiority, the Romans subdued all other states and cowed their own citizens. The Pax Romana came down to this: a privileged elite enjoyed immense wealth and exercised power with little accountability to the masses. The vast majority of people lived in five-story walkups and struggled to put ramen noodles on the dinner table. The ruling class brutally suppressed attempts to change the social order in favor of what they saw as the nobodies. Think crucifixion, for instance. For that matter, Paul endured his own share of personal hardships. He was beaten, stoned, slandered, shipwrecked, snake-bit, and imprisoned. Eventually, the Romans beheaded him. And yet, Paul encouraged his fledgling congregations not to lose hope. That hope, he says, will not disappoint them (Romans 5:5).

In his day, the same old self-centered tribes still surrounded his fledgling little tribe. Today, violence and oppression, exploitation and poverty still mar human life. In some seasons, like our own, these dehumanizing forces seem to be gathering strength. We have seen children and teachers slaughtered in their classrooms. Disgruntled citizens have opened fire on elected officials. Nightclubs have become shooting galleries. Thousands of American troops are still sent to Afghanistan after more than a decade of war. Terrorists in Great Britain have bombed concert goers and driven their vehicles into crowds of unsuspecting pedestrians. We're experiencing a sharp rise in violence against ethnic minorities, non-Christian religious groups, and members of the LGBTQ community.

But Paul would also remind us not to despair. Hope does not disappoint so long as we feed the hungry and shelter the homeless. So long as we refuse to greet the stranger as an enemy. So long as we insist that our own welfare depends upon our neighbor's well-being. So long as we not only respect but guard the dignity of every human being. When Paul said that hope doesn't disappoint, I think he was getting at something like this: Don't just cling to hope. Be it. Lead a resurrection-shaped life.

And that is just what Collette is doing. Collette is pursuing a dream that, as it turns out, points remarkably toward a New Heaven and a New Earth. She seeks more than a paycheck; she wants to form a company where people who have faced challenges, rejection, struggles, and prejudice discover their value and know that they are indispensable. You might assume that Collette wants to employ people like her, but you would be missing the deeper point. She envisions a company that will hire people not because they are like her or anyone else in the firm. It will be a company where anyone and everyone belongs. A place where everyone fits. Everybody she meets is one of us. She doesn't divide the world into us and them. There's just us. Learning to make room for each other is crucial to leading a resurrection-shaped life.

Making Room for One More

They said it was going to be a retreat. I was skeptical. Retreats offer spiritual exercises and spans of quiet time designed to nurture insight and to encourage renewal. By contrast, our weekend together was shaping up to be a bloodletting.

The vestry and clergy of our large suburban parish gathered at a Methodist conference center for what was billed as a time of visioning led by a highly paid consultant. Along with polo shirts and Bermuda shorts, some participants dragged along seething resentments and others smuggled in poorly concealed anxieties. Tensions between the rector and the lay leadership had been mounting since before I arrived as a newly minted priest the previous summer. A couple of assisting priests and I were loyal to our rector. We recognized that he struggled with administrative tasks and delivered sloppy sermons. His vision for the parish was vague and uninspiring. And yet, we loved him. He was genuinely kind and nurturing, generous and good-humored.

The morning unfolded with two increasingly rocky sessions. The unstated agenda among a strong core of the vestry was to announce their disappointment with the rector's performance. There was bitter acrimony in the air from the beginning. The message was clear: the rector was incompetent, and the consultant's fee was an exorbitant waste of money.

At the lunch break, members of the vestry stalked directly to the dining hall. Along with the other assisting clergy, I loitered with the rector. He had taken a beating. We wanted to make sure he still had a pulse and to reassure him that we still loved him.

As I emerged from the cafeteria line and looked for a place to sit, I noticed the vestry sitting at a large round table. I made my way there only to see that all the seats had already been taken. Every head turned my way. Some faces bore an embarrassed expression, others uncertainty and mistrust. A couple of people gave me the stink eye. No one offered to make space for me at the table. Somebody muttered that they were all about to leave anyway. There was some awkward shuffling, but nobody moved. Finally I said, "Don't worry about it. I can just sit right over here." I sat alone at an adjacent table.

This memory came back to me when I read a very different dining hall story by Diana Butler Bass. Early in her freshman year at college, Diana carried her tray into the school's vast dining hall searching for a place to sit. The room was filled with unfamiliar faces and the chatter of people already in comfortably established groups. Then someone she had met at orientation called out for her to join her. When Diana got to the table, she saw that all the seats were taken. As Diana began to turn away to another table, her new friend started pushing plates aside to make a space for her. "There's always room for one more," she said.[4]

There is always room for one more—but we still have to make space for her. For them. I had known each of these vestry members before that wretched retreat and awkward lunch experience. We liked each other well enough. In fact, I had grown close to some of them. All of them were good, kind, generous people. And yet, they couldn't make room that day.

As I look back on it, I realize that all of us come to a place where making room for one more seems not only unattractive but also downright hazardous. As a result, we build walls to protect us from them. Behind those walls we shrink and wither, neglect others, and diminish ourselves with the very barriers that we thought would make us safe and strong. So it is especially instructive for us to read that Jesus identifies himself as a gate (John 10:7-9). But it would not be surprising if you had missed hearing Jesus speak about himself in these terms. He says it in the midst of the chapter in John's Gospel where he also says, "I am the good shepherd" (John 10:11). Countless preachers and teachers have invited us to imagine Jesus as a gentle shepherd carrying a lamb on his shoulders. Kitschy artists and artisans could not have asked for a better subject. Sweet Jesus carries each of us as his precious lambs. But instead of the comforting image of the Good Shepherd, I ask you to focus on the odd, unromantic image of Jesus as the gate in the sheep pen. He says, "I am the gate" (John 10:9). Jesus is more interested in gates than he is in walls.

We build plenty of walls. That's our problem. What we need is a gate.

Many of us remember the adage, "Good fences make good neighbors." And maybe you're thinking something like that right now. That phrase came to many of us from Robert Frost's familiar poem, "Mending Wall." And there's an irony—and perhaps a fearful resistance—at work when we recall it. You see, we're either unwittingly or deliberately recalling it out of context.

As Diana Butler Bass reminds us, the poem deliberately and artfully calls the virtue of building walls into question.[5] Listen to the first line of Frost's poem: "Something there is that doesn't love a wall." As the two men collect and stack the tumbled rocks, one man begins to wonder about the wisdom of such a wall in the first place. After all, a pine forest grows on his neighbor's land. An apple orchard grows on his. They are building the wall just for the sake of separation. Pines and apple trees don't pose a threat to one another.

The second man utters the phrase about fences and neighbors unreflectively. It's what he learned as a child, I suppose. He remains untroubled by his neighbor's musings. His words fall upon deaf ears. And yet, there remains something that doesn't love a wall. The frozen rain and the shifting earth, the burrowing rabbits and the frantic beagles never stop their work. Ragged gaps keep tumbling open by a force that neither neighbor can resist or eradicate. The question is only this: Will they have the courage to pass through that gap? To welcome others as they pass through? Or will they scramble again and again to shore up their walls?

Jesus doesn't say that he is the sheep pen. He is the gate through which the sheep can come and go. Later in the chapter he adds, "I have other sheep that do not belong to this fold" (John 10:16). And yet he wants one flock, not a confederacy of separate sheep pens. Those many folds—all of those us-versus-them divisions maintained by the walls we build—will become one flock only if the sheep pass freely through the gate.

So, whenever we find ourselves sitting comfortably at our accustomed place at table—or in the office or on the playing field or in the classroom or in the neighborhood—Christ bids us to remember that every table, every human gathering, can be an image of the Eucharistic table, the table at the Great Banquet. It is actually not our table; even the most humble table stands for Christ's Holy Table. We might see our table as full, but Jesus sees things differently. There's always room for one more. You might just need to shove some of your plates aside, and open your heart, to make space.

Being Together

Just because you're sitting next to people at the dinner table doesn't mean you're actually close to them. Take, for instance, my memory of the time Joy and I shared Thanksgiving dinner with my father, his wife, and his in-laws from that marriage.

Joy and I had tied the knot three years earlier. We were living in Rocky Mount, North Carolina. She taught in a social services program at nearby Edgecomb Tech. I held a position on the North Carolina Wesleyan faculty. We dutifully, if unenthusiastically, drove the five-and-a-half hours to tiny Louisville, Georgia. Louisville's quiet Main Street offered no diversions from what we imagined would be an immersion experience in family dysfunction.

Thanksgiving arrived. Eight of us gathered around a six-person table jammed into one side of an already cramped living room. My father, his wife, her sister, her sister's husband, their two adult children, Joy, and I sat with arms close to our sides. Elbows were nearly brushing elbows.

It's entirely possible that somebody said the blessing. It felt more like somebody had fired a starting pistol. Individuals were grabbing serving dishes near them and standing to reach across the table for more distant dishes. They were all hurriedly plopping mashed potatoes, green beans, dressing, asparagus casserole, and turkey on their plates as quickly as they could. No one passed anything around the table. It was each person for himself or herself.

Dazed, I eventually reached for a nearby roll and snatched a bit of turkey from a plate that happened to land close by. Looking across the table I saw Joy's empty plate and the appalled look on her face. No one else noticed. They were too busy eating. I offered a silent, heartfelt prayer of thanks that we hadn't done this before we had gotten married.

My father and his brother-in-law dominated the conversation that followed the first rush of eating. I recall not a single thing they talked about. The volume of my inner voice was too high. It was saying something like, *Can we leave the table yet? Is it time to drive home? Will Joy ever speak to me again?*

Joy and I have spent every Thanksgiving together since then. Somewhere else.

Sitting next to each other around a table is pretty easy. Gravity does most of the work. Being together, *really* being together, can be challenging. Grace does most of that work. But grace requires our cooperation. God, apparently, is up for and up to the challenge of bringing us—all of us—together in more than merely spatial contiguity. God will settle for nothing less than genuine intimacy. Jesus makes this point with a parable often called the parable of the wedding feast or the parable of the great banquet (Matthew 22:1-14).

A king holds a feast to celebrate his son's wedding. Nobody on the first invitation list RSVPs. So Dad expands the list. His servants stand at the entrance of Walmart, hand out flyers at intersections, and flood social media with memes containing date, time, and place for anybody who wants to show up. If you don't show, you'll completely miss out and really regret it.

Once the party got started, the king came into the hall to greet his guests. He quickly noticed that one of the people attending the feast had not bothered to wear a wedding robe. This guest had accepted the invitation, but he wasn't putting forth the effort to genuinely take part in the celebration. Summoning his servants, the king ordered them to usher the ill-dressed guest out the door.

Merely showing up is not enough; you have to really be present to the people you're with. Jesus summed it up like this, "For many are called, but few are chosen" (Matthew 22:14).

Keep in mind that this is a parable, not an allegory. As I explained earlier, listening to parables opens us to new perspectives and expands our horizons. As it turns out, this parable teaches us significant lessons about human relationships and about encountering the holy right here on planet Earth. God created all that is out of nothing. God had no interest in making pretty things to admire from a distance or a toy to wind up and watch go. And regardless of what you may have heard, God's purpose in the creation was not to see if human beings could measure up to God's moral standards. God brought everything to be in order to enjoy perfect, inseparable intimacy with each and every being and for every being to be in harmony with all others. For God it will never be enough that we merely take up space next to each other on this planet.

God yearns for us to take up space in each other's hearts. That is how God encounters us and we encounter God. In and through our love for each other. Showing up to the feast with the wrong clothing—no shirt, no shoes—is something like just sitting at the table but being somewhere else in our hearts and minds and souls. In Jesus, we see that God wants nothing less than for us to be together. *Really* be together. And in being together, we will be together with our Maker. Nevertheless, stretching toward this kind of togetherness can be very risky. We won't get there by playing it safe.

Do Something

John Lewis is a prominent civil rights leader and now serves as US Representative for Georgia. Fifty-six years ago, as a relatively unknown African American man, Lewis used a whites-only restroom in Jackson, Mississippi. Police arrested him, and authorities sent him to Parchman Prison. Parchman is the state's only maximum-security prison for men. Lewis entered that restroom to protest racism in America. He knew that arrest and imprisonment would probably follow. In the segregated South, black men, women, and even children had been lynched for less. For the sake of justice, Lewis willingly endured this brutal, demeaning treatment. As we discussed in chapter 2, a higher purpose propelled and clarified Lewis's life. His devotion to civil rights gave him the courage to take risks and to suffer pain and hardship.

In the last century and in the current century, many people who have been faced with similar choices and analogous risks have hesitated. They have considered the potentially negative consequences of their actions and weighed those consequences against what they perceive to be the negligible effect that their small actions could have on so vast a social problem. Lewis may have made the same sort of mental calculation. And he chose to act. He was under no illusion that his act in isolation—violating a Jim Crow law in the Deep South on this single occasion—would suddenly dismantle the legal, political, and social structures that were and are systemic racism. However, his abiding and motivating faith was that his actions would be woven together by God with the actions of thousands of other people he might never know. He did not have the power to do everything, but his actions that day would form part of a great, holy wave, and he understood that he did have the power to make a difference. Congressman Lewis learned this truth from Jesus. And so should we. Just because we can't do everything doesn't mean that we shouldn't do something.

Consider Mark's account of Jesus's day in Capernaum (Mark 1:29-39). Having just wowed the crowd at the local synagogue, Jesus makes his way with Andrew and Simon Peter to Peter's house. As it turns out, Peter's mother-in-law is bedridden with fever. No sooner does Jesus heal her than the whole town swarms the place looking for cures for every kind of ailment and for exorcisms of a variety of chatty demons. Many were healed and made demon-free by bedtime. Apparently, there was still a long waiting line of sick and possessed people early the next day. Jesus had not healed everybody in Capernaum. And it was time to move on.

Jesus did the good that he could do that day. And then he moved on to do the good that he could do on a new day. He healed many people and removed spiritual burdens from others. Yes, many others still suffered. But Jesus refused to be overwhelmed or frozen into inactivity by the enormity of the challenge before him.

Healing stories and exorcisms make up one third of Mark's Gospel. That's more than the space that Mark allots to the Passion Narrative. And Mark must have had a reason for shaping his version of Jesus's life in this way. I suspect that Mark wanted us to understand that the gospel is not a list of concepts to which we assent. Neither is it a moral code to which we adhere. The gospel is a power unleashed on this earth through feeble hands like yours and mine. The gospel is something we do. Well, actually, the gospel is something that God does through us. God will raise the entire creation to new life, but not without us. As it turns out, to follow Jesus we have to do something. When we do nothing, we are actually adding to the misery and injustice of this world.

But let's be honest. It is easy to grow discouraged when the tide seems to be rising against us. Our best efforts sometimes seem to come to nothing. John the Baptist faced a crisis like this (Matthew 11:2-3). After Jesus's ministry had gotten serious traction, John the Baptist found himself languishing in prison. It's bad enough to be stuck in Herod's moldy, rat-infested basement, but John realized that he wouldn't leave the palace grounds with his head attached. John's blunt criticisms of the establishment and his fierce confrontations with the rich and powerful had landed him in a cell. He had called Israel to a better way. A way that he believed right down to his sandals was God's way. After all, he had gotten it from Scripture. Love your neighbor as yourself. Care for the widow and the orphan. Do not enrich yourself at the expense of others. Oppress no one with force of arms and the threat of violence. Welcome the stranger and the foreigner. Ensure that all people have a way to make a decent life for themselves. For his efforts, he was rotting in jail and facing a grisly execution.

Staring at the walls and fighting back images of the chopping block, John started wondering, *Was it worth it?* And so, he sends his followers to Jesus. He wants to know, "Are you the one?" Is God really going to make justice happen? Or am I suffering for nothing? (Matthew 11:3). Jesus answers by pointing to his works. "The blind receive their sight, the lame walk, the lepers are cleansed, the deaf hear, the dead are raised, and the poor have good news brought to them" (Matthew 11:5).

I take his meaning to be something like this: Would your life be worth living if you didn't do whatever it takes to pursue the dream of God's justice for all? Sister Helen Prejean once Tweeted about a conversation she had with a member of an execution strap-down team. He said to her, "What am I supposed to tell my kids when I get home?"[6] Later, the man quit the job. Sure, you could have played it safe. You might save your life by keeping your mouth shut. By going along to get along. But in a more significant sense, you would lose your life. You would become a tormented soul. Filled with regret and fear and shame.

Paradoxically, devoting ourselves to God's healing work in the world allows us to live comfortably in our own skin, even when the world brands us as clowns, fools, and losers for it. Conversely, forsaking the dream of new life for a paycheck, social approval, or personal safety withers the soul. Jesus urges us to follow him on the way of the cross. It is the only way to inhabit a resurrection-shaped life.

REFLECTION QUESTIONS

1. What idea, image, story, or passage from this chapter grabbed your attention or captured your imagination? How does it connect with or differ from your own experiences of belonging and being excluded?
2. Talk about a time that you felt like you belonged.
3. Share a story about a time that you felt excluded.
4. Think of some ways that you divide the world into us and them. What are some of the challenges in overcoming that division in your life?
5. Have you ever paid a price for speaking up about or resisting an injustice? Has fear of consequences ever made you hesitate to take action against injustice? Tell the story.

POSTLUDE

New life starts in the dark. Whether it is a seed in the ground, a baby in the womb, or Jesus in the tomb, it starts in the dark.

—Barbara Brown Taylor, *Learning to Walk in the Dark*

We are what we have grown beyond. That's what it means to inhabit a resurrection-shaped life. Whether we are recovering from personal failures, finding joy after great sorrow, or mending a fractured relationship, we are people who have died and risen. An old life has passed away and a new life emerges. Resurrection begins on planet Earth. And while some may be content to think of resurrection as merely a metaphor for how humans change and grow, I believe that the fullness of the resurrection awaits us after our lungs have drawn their last breath and our hearts have ceased to beat. The resurrection-shaped life we lead in our ordinary comings and goings foreshadows life beyond this life.

My belief in life beyond death is more than an adherence to a church doctrine or a philosophical conclusion I have drawn. It is true that my thoughts about life after death have been influenced by the church's teachings, by the writings of great theologians like Thomas Aquinas and Karl Rahner, and by the arguments of philosophers from Plato to Kierkegaard. But my belief arises from something more personal and visceral. All my reading and reflection have, in the end, helped me unpack the meaning of an experience I had as a young child: the death of my little sister Marie when I was three.[1]

My mom sought to soften the blow for me, and perhaps for herself, by telling me that Marie was in heaven. Her words gave me a child's simple way of articulating how I could at once feel my sister's absence and continue to have a sense of connection with her. Over time, the dual experience of my sister's absence and our connection—and now that same experience with my mother and my maternal grandparents—has continued to stir my theological imagination.

In college and graduate school, I drifted intellectually between agnosticism and atheism. All the while, my heart continued to nurture the hope that there was something more to life than meets the eye. As I was completing my doctoral studies in philosophy, my studies of human consciousness provided me the intellectual tools I needed to begin unpacking what my heart knew in its own way. My Christian faith gradually re-emerged. By the time I had secured a tenure-track position in the academic world, my commitment to sacramental practices had become habitual and spiritually sustaining. Nevertheless, I was still trying to make intellectual sense of the Christian faith. So, at a meeting of the American Philosophical Association, I approached one of my favorite teachers to talk about it. Tom is an expert in contemporary continental philosophy and also a Roman Catholic priest. He affirmed his own belief in life after death. And while Tom didn't launch into a long monologue, he said enough to remind me that resurrection is not the same thing as what philosophers call the immortality of the soul. And that's a crucial distinction for understanding the idea of a resurrection-shaped life.

Paradise Misunderstood

As I mentioned above, my mother probably sought to soften the blow of my sister's death by telling me that she had gone to heaven. She was motivated by kindness and a mother's desire to protect her only surviving child. Whether she meant to impart a theological idea to me or not, I came away with one. And the theological concept of the afterlife that I gathered from her words is the immortality of the soul.

The Bible does not teach the immortality of the soul. We have received it from Greek philosophy. According to this view, the body houses the soul. In fact, some philosophers have considered the body the soul's prison. When we draw our last breath, the soul escapes the body and continues to live for eternity. The disembodied soul is the real you. Even though the Gospel stories clearly tell us that Jesus rose bodily—and I'll get to what that means below—many Christians still think about death as the flight of a disembodied soul from this world to some other place.

Christians influenced by the Greek concept of immortality then often graft onto it the idea of eternal judgment. Good souls go to heaven. Bad souls go to hell. Or, more precisely, souls that have claimed Jesus as Lord and Savior pass through the pearly gates. All other souls suffer eternal torment. Heaven is synonymous with paradise. In other words, life after death is about a change of celestial address. *Where* we are changes, not *who* we are. Paradise is the place we never suffer or worry or work. In paradise, we enjoy the pleasures of this life uninterrupted by life's sorrows and drudgery. For instance, I once heard a person say he can't wait to get to heaven, because he would be duck hunting all the time. I smiled and nodded and thought, *Not much of a heaven for the ducks.*

This view of life after death is a misunderstanding of paradise. It focuses on where we will go instead of who we are becoming. By contrast, the resurrection teaches us that God transforms who we are through a continual process of dying and rising. We are what we have overcome. Unto eternity. Since the word *heaven* is so frequently associated with this idea of paradise, I usually avoid using the word *heaven* when I talk about life after death. Nevertheless, it will be instructive to revisit the Bible story that some assume conveys the message that humans had once enjoyed and then lost paradise: the story of the garden of Eden (Genesis 2:4-3:24).

In the beginning, God created a garden and placed Adam and Eve in it. Their role was to tend and to nurture that garden. The trees and the bushes bore all the fruit they needed to survive, and God gave them permission to eat whatever they wanted with one exception. The fruit of the Tree of the Knowledge of Good and Evil was off limits. This was paradise. No toil. No fear. No competition. No suffering. And then things took the famously bad turn. God expelled Adam and Eve from the garden of Eden after they ate from the forbidden tree. Paradise was lost.

Many read this story and understandably assume that the first couple's expulsion from the garden was God's punishment for their disobedience. Reading the story this way frames their view of the afterlife. Getting into heaven is like a return to the paradise we were meant to enjoy in the first place. I suggest a different reading. The expulsion is not a punishment for eating the forbidden fruit. There are consequences. Life will be filled with toil and struggle and sorrow. However, the expulsion immediately follows a conclusion that God draws about Adam and Eve once they've eaten of the Tree of the Knowledge of Good and Evil. God sends them from the Garden and bars their return after realizing that they might eat of the Tree of Life and live forever. On the face of it, this seems incongruously petty for the Creator. But a closer look helps us get the message more clearly.

Adam and Eve are already experiencing the unavoidable consequences of a life shaped by the pursuit of material comfort and pleasure: toil, deception, manipulation, competition, frustration, and alienation. In other words, they now know not only the gap between how life could be and how life actually is, but they also seem to have settled for the latter so long as they could keep consuming whatever they want. If they ate of the Tree of Life, they would simply go on like this forever. A life of suffering, anxiety, and striving would go on endlessly. One miserable thing after another. This is not eternal life. It's perpetual life in an illusory paradise, in a place where we get everything we want. However, life beyond death is not a place where we get everything we want. It's the life permeated by God and animated by love for everyone we meet. In other words, we can reclaim the idea of "paradise" if we recognize that it is a way of living. A resurrection-shaped life replaces the illusion of an eternally carefree life with the scriptural vision of an inexhaustibly caring life.

Inexhaustible Caring

As I explained above, when we think of life beyond death as paradise, we may imagine it to be an eternally carefree life. Ironically, a carefree life comes much closer to hell than to heaven. That's one of the lessons that Jesus conveys in what is frequently called the parable of the talents (Matthew 25:14-30). It goes like this.

Before going on a long journey, a man charges three slaves with taking care of a portion of his property. Assessing their relative abilities, the man gives one slave about $75,000, another $30,000, and the final slave $15,000. That was five talents, two talents, and one talent in the money of the day. When the master returns, the first two slaves return the original investments with enviable returns. They took risks to make more of what they had been given to start with. The third slave hands back the one talent or $15,000 he was given, reporting that he had buried the master's money. The master responds by exiling the third slave to the outer darkness.

Remember that parables stimulate our reflection and encourage us to revisit our habitual ways of seeing things. Parables stretch our souls and broaden our perceptions rather than filling us with facts and concepts. In the case of the parable of the talents, leave aside the frequent assumption that the master represents Jesus at the Second Coming. Instead, let the story be a spiritual puzzle.

Take a look at what the third slave says to the returning master. "Master, I knew that you were a harsh man, reaping where you did not sow, and gathering where you did not scatter seed; so I was afraid, and I went and hid your talent in the ground. Here you have what is yours" (Matthew 25:24-25). The third slave sought to live a blameless life. As a result, he projected a blaming posture onto the master. Further, his blame circled back and crushed him. The only path to blamelessness is to be uncaring. To care is to invest in what's going on around you, to take risks, to suffer loss, to be accountable, and to commit. The third slave sought to escape accountability and to detach from the world. He sought to be carefree, that is to say, without a care in this world.

Imagine for a minute what it would really mean to say that you don't have a care in the world. Or, better yet, let Jesus show us by way of another parable. People frequently call it the parable of the rich fool (Luke 12:16-21). Jesus says that a farmer brought in a bumper crop. His first thought was to store the excess for his own private use. In fact, he had to build additional silos to hold all the grain. The extra he had accumulated would support an early retirement and a life of leisure. Focusing solely on his own comfort and security, the farmer ignored the need, the suffering, and the insecurity all around him. He didn't have a care in the world because he only cared about himself.

On the very night that the last new silo was stuffed to its ceiling, the farmer died. The parable concludes with God's own response to the farmer: "You fool! This very night your life is being demanded of you. And the things you have prepared, whose will they be?" (Luke 12:20). In other words, the farmer has utterly missed the point of human existence. Life centered on caring for ourselves turns to dust. A life devoted to the growth, nurture, and well-being of others stretches into eternity. A resurrection-shaped life is love in the flesh.

Maybe the farmer thought, *I deserve this. I worked hard for it.* Or maybe he looked at the poor and thought, *It's not my fault. I didn't make them poor. They're lazy.* In either case, the farmer assumes that his principal concern is his own life. Tending to the well-being of others is an optional add-on to life, not its animating spirit. And he could not be more mistaken.

The parable of the talents—along with the parable of the rich fool—is an end-of-the-day parable. I'm not sure where I first heard that phrase, "at the end of the day." But I do remember that one of my former professors frequently used it. He would preface a remark with the phrase meaning that he was about to sum up the meaning of a passage of Scripture or a theological concept. "This is what it all comes down to," he would be saying. And so an end-of-the-day parable nudges us to ask these questions: What's the point of all this? Why am I here? What am I to do with my life in order for this life to make any sense at all?

The third slave and the foolish rich man seem to be working for the celestial weekend. Perhaps unwittingly, they strive to get to the point where nothing matters anymore. Nothing, that is, except for their own comfort and security. Jesus points in a very different direction. He points to a resurrection-shaped life. Life is not about being endlessly carefree. It's about being unguardedly, relentlessly caring. At the end of the day, our tears will be wiped away (Isaiah 25:8; Revelation 7:17; 21:4). But the point is that we have shed tears. Tears of love. We have not protected ourselves from pain and sorrow and loss. God does not merely erase our tears as the relics of a forgotten past. In the resurrection, our tears and even our death are what we will have grown beyond once and for all. This is what we learn in the Gospel accounts of the resurrection of Jesus.

Life and Death and Life

Jesus passed through death once and for all to a radically new kind of life. In other words, Jesus did not merely come back from the dead to pick up where he had left off. That would be more properly called a resuscitation. Lazarus came back from the dead. Or rather, Jesus resuscitated him so that he could resume life as usual. At some point in the future Lazarus faced the end of this biological life once again.

God gave Jesus new life. Jesus did not give it to himself. After all, he couldn't give himself anything. He was dead as a doornail. The dead don't pull themselves up by their own bootstraps. You see, resurrection can happen only once there is no hope of reviving the old life that we had worked so hard to build and sustain. The path to Easter always passes through Good Friday.

Jesus is risen. And he is imparting his new life to us—to you and to me—as we stumble and scurry and skip and dance and scooch our way along our various paths. One day, our earthly lives will come to an end, and we will fully inhabit the new life imparted by Christ. For now, we are growing into eternal life gradually, one day—sometimes one moment—at a time. Growing into eternal life is not something we achieve. We can't speed it up by trying harder or getting the hang of it. Eternal life doesn't even come as a reward for good conduct, exemplary spiritual practices, or exceptional faith. We just have to die. And then God gives us eternal life. As a gift. Those of us who choose to follow Jesus intentionally walk a path punctuated by dying and rising.

Before we draw our last breaths, we will from time to time meet what you might call smaller deaths. None of these deaths will be our final moment, but they will be real and unavoidable. The life that we have grown so accustomed to and worked with such love and sweat to nurture and tend grinds to a halt or shatters or evaporates or grows unbearably hollow. We will certainly mourn that good life. For some time, we'll struggle to admit that the life we knew is no more. We may resist the very idea that it's gone, trying again and again to revive it. All to no avail.

I experienced that sort of death as a child when my parents divorced. The death of a loved one or the end of a relationship can shatter a life. Our bodies age us into new seasons of living. Good things like graduation from high school and college mark the end of a pattern of life. We have to let go of the old life in order to take up and grow accustomed to the new life we've been given. Sometimes we enter that new life with such joy that we hardly notice the grief, but this is not always true. Sometimes, our sorrow is so deep that we can't imagine any new life at all.

That's how we find Mary Magdalene on the day of resurrection (John 20:11-18). Well, for her, it was the third day since her world had come to an end. Racked with grief, she was going through the motions of an old life robbed forever of all its former light and laughter. Jesus had been at the center of her world. And without its center, that once glittering, orderly world had become a heap of dusty rubble.

Jesus chose to show himself first of all to Mary Magdalene. And he wasn't content to just show himself. He took pains to teach her what it means to give herself to the resurrection power of God's love. "Don't cling to me," he said. In other words, don't cling to the me I used to be, to the life we used to have.

Mary imagined for just a moment that Jesus was back from the dead. They could pick up where they had left off. The life she feared she had lost was restored. At least, that's what she thought. But Jesus was not back from the dead; he had passed through death to new life. Magdalene's old life—the life that she shared with Jesus and the other disciples—was over. He came to give her, them, and the rest of us a new life.

Jesus was teaching Mary Magdalene to cling to the risen Christ. And as difficult and painful as it would be, Mary had to let go of that old life to begin—step by step—to inhabit the new life that Jesus was bringing her. Letting go of the old life can be very hard, and it is also true that we will spend some time feeling awkward and disoriented in the new life that Christ is giving us. Feeling at home in eternal life takes time and no little amount of trial and error.

The very essence of eternal life is love. Eternal life reflects the very heart of the God who imparts it. As it turns out, getting the hang of eternal life involves growing into a life of habitual love. God's love is not a mere response to circumstances. It is a free and creative force that enters unlooked-for into the unlikeliest of places. Love's presence raises up what has been cast down, makes new what has grown old, and brings all things to perfection in Christ, through whom all things were made.

Love has died to judging others for being different and embraces each person and every creature as the beloved child of God. Love has died to the drive to get ahead and devotes itself to leaving no one behind. Love has died to seeking its own status and guards the dignity of every human being. Love has died to settling scores to make things right and forgives to restore right relationships. Love has died to comfort and personal privilege and pursues justice for the forgotten and the persecuted, the despised and the oppressed.

Jesus did not come back from the dead. He passed through death to eternal life. And that is the pattern we follow when we emulate Christ. We die to a narrow life that we have known and rise to a new and wider life. This is a resurrection-shaped life. And the hope that draws such a life forward is that, in Christ, we too will have grown beyond sorrow, pain, regret, and death once and for all.

ACKNOWLEDGMENTS

From one perspective, this book began with a phone call from Susan Salley of Abingdon Press. She asked, "What are you working on right now?" In retrospect it seems to me that I rambled about one thing and another before realizing that I was talking about the meaning of the resurrection in our ordinary, everyday lives. Her enthusiasm persuaded me to turn those thoughts into the book that you are reading now. I am indebted to her for her early encouragement and confidence in me.

Christina Boys devoted boundless energy and remarkable talent to transforming the manuscript I submitted into the book that you have before you today. Her editorial guidance sharpened my prose and clarified my thoughts. I am immensely grateful. Brenda Smotherman's marketing skills connected me to the reading community who would find my work most meaningful. I give thanks for her rich imagination and indispensable assistance in finding ways to reach my readers. Finally, my thanks go out to Susan Cornell for shepherding this work through the production phase. The elegant, professional form of this text is a tribute to her skill and patient dedication.

Writing is a daily spiritual practice for me. So, when Susan raised her question, I was scrambling to crystallize weeks upon weeks of journal entries, some of which have appeared at my blog "Looking for God in Messy Places." My readers and I are participating in a long and winding conversation. Their responses at my blog, via email, and on social media continue to shape and motivate my reflections. My affection for these readers is a gift, and my gratitude to them is deep.

Members of my staff have been immensely supportive of the writing aspect of my broader ministry as a bishop in The Episcopal Church. In their way, Canon Bill Bryant and Dean Ron Clingenpeel nudged me to give myself permission to spend the time and energy in writing. Their friendship and wisdom make it easier for me to delegate to them the crucial and often trying ministries of congregational vitality and clergy deployment. We worked as a team, each applying our gifts to the challenges and the tasks to which we are best suited. Holly Davis, Kathy Richey, and Joy Owensby are equally vital members of this team. Their expert management of day-to-day administrative operations, diocesan program development and oversight, and my schedule and travel arrangements makes it possible for me to focus on spiritual leadership and theological reflection. I am grateful to all of these colleagues for helping me be a bishop who writes. And I owe thanks to my spiritual director Dennis Campbell for encouraging me to see the value that being this kind of bishop offers the broader church.

Finally, I am especially grateful to and for my family. Conversations with our sons Patrick and Andrew have deepened my understanding of repentance, overcoming loss, and dealing with sorrow. Meredith, our daughter, continues to teach me about inclusive community, belonging, and the healing power of a compassionate heart. Joy is my soul friend. On our morning walks and in our evening talks, we frequently go to deep and tender places, and her discerning ear and insightful reflections helped refine many of the ideas in this book. Without her, those ideas would have remained a tangled mess of images and vague thoughts. Her reading of the manuscript was crucial to its completion. As I said in the dedication at the beginning of this book, she is my most favorite person ever.

NOTES

Prelude

1. Marcus Borg, *The Heart of Christianity: Rediscovering a Life of Faith* (New York: HarperCollins, 2003), 107–19.

2. Anne Lamott, *Hallelujah Anyway: Rediscovering Mercy* (New York: Riverhead Books, 2017), 48. Lamott identifies the art form as Chinese.

3. "Mending Fragile Things," June 16, 2017, twliii.com, https://twliii.com/2017/06/16/mending-fragile-things/.

2. The Meaning of Suffering

1. *Night and Fog* (originally *Nuit et brouillard*) is a French documentary short film (1956) directed by Alain Resnais.

2. Viktor E. Frankl, *Man's Search for Meaning*, part 1 trans. Ilsa Lasch (Boston: Beacon, 2006).

3. Sara Miles, "By Water and By Fire," blog post, http://saramiles.net/articles/1.

4. Miles, "By Water and By Fire."

5. Miles, "By Water and By Fire."

6. Miles, "By Water and By Fire."

7. Becky Garrison, "So Dang Jesus-y: Sara Miles' *Jesus Freak*," *Sojourners*, February 22, 2010, https://sojo.net/articles/so-dang-jesus-y-sara-miles-jesus-freak.

8. Malcom Gladwell, *Outliers: The Story of Success* (Boston: Little, Brown and Company, 2008), 35–68.

9. Mark Manson, *The Subtle Art of Not Giving a F*ck: The Counterintuitive Approach to Living a Good Life* (New York: HarperOne, 2016), 63–86.

3. Recovering from Shame and Blame

1. Brené Brown, *The Gifts of Imperfection: Let Go of Who You Think You Are Supposed to Be and Embrace Who You Are* (Center City, MN: Hazelden, 2009), 15–18.

2. Brown, *Gifts of Imperfection*, 7–11.

3. Reza Aslan, *God: A Human History* (New York: Random House, 2017).

4. Mending Loss and Sorrow

1. Kazuo Ishiguro, *Never Let Me Go* (New York: Vintage, 2005), 60.

2. American Academy of Bereavement, "Unconditional Grief: Grieving Someone Alive," October 20, 2015, http://thebereavementacademy.com/unconventional-grief-grieving-someone-alive/.

5. Forgiveness, Passion, and Justice

1. Thordis Elva and Tom Stranger, "Our Story of Rape and Reconciliation," TEDWomen, October 2016, www.ted.com/talks/thordis_elva_tom_stranger_our_story_of_rape_and_reconciliation.

2. Henri Nouwen, *The Wounded Healer* (New York: Doubleday, 1979).

3. Henri Nouwen, "The Wounded Healer" meditation, July 8, 2017, http://henrinouwen.org/meditation/the-wounded-healer/.

4. Ronald Rolheiser, "Social Justice—New Knowledge/New Responsibility," April 15, 1991, http://ronrolheiser.com/social-justice-new-knowledgenew-responsibility/#.W3byDY73-IY.

5. Lauren F. Winner, *Wearing God: Clothing, Laughter, Fire and Other*

Overlooked Ways of Meeting God (New York: HarperCollins, 2015), Kindle location 2567.

6. Just Us

1. See Collette's website at www.colletteys.com.

2. Annie Dillard, *Pilgrim at Tinker Creek* (New York: HarperCollins, 1974), 17.

3. Diana Butler Bass, *Grounded: Finding God in the Word—A Spiritual Revolution* (New York: HarperCollins, 2015), 209–14; Brian McLaren, *The Great Spiritual Migration: How the World's Largest Religion Is Seeking a Better Way to Be Christian* (New York: Convergent, 2016), 70–88.

4. Butler Bass, *Grounded*, 240.

5. Butler Bass, *Grounded*, 215.

6. Helen Prejean (@helenprejean), "What am I supposed to tell my kids," Twitter, July 6, 2017, 6:43 p.m.

Postlude

1. I have discussed Marie's death from different perspectives in two of my previous works: *Gospel Memories: The Future Can Rewrite Our Past* (New York: Morehouse, 2016), 40–45; *Your Untold Story: Tales of a Child of God* (New York: Church Publishing, 2018), 73–76.